DEMOCRACY IN DECLINE

SAGE was founded in 1965 by Sara Miller McCune to support the dissemination of usable knowledge by publishing innovative and high-quality research and teaching content. Today, we publish over 900 journals, including those of more than 400 learned societies, more than 800 new books per year, and a growing range of library products including archives, data, case studies, reports, and video. SAGE remains majority-owned by our founder, and after Sara's lifetime will become owned by a charitable trust that secures our continued independence.

Los Angeles | London | New Delhi | Singapore | Washington DC | Melbourne

DEMOCRACY IN DECLINE

Rebuilding its future

PHILIP KOTLER

Los Angeles | London | New Delhi
Singapore | Washington DC | Melbourne

Los Angeles | London | New Delhi
Singapore | Washington DC

SAGE Publications Ltd
1 Oliver's Yard
55 City Road
London EC1Y 1SP

SAGE Publications Inc.
2455 Teller Road
Thousand Oaks, California 91320

SAGE Publications India Pvt Ltd
B 1/I 1 Mohan Cooperative Industrial Area
Mathura Road
New Delhi 110 044

SAGE Publications Asia-Pacific Pte Ltd
3 Church Street
#10-04 Samsung Hub
Singapore 049483

Editor: Matthew Waters
Editorial assistant: Lyndsay Aitken
Production editor: Nicola Marshall
Copyeditor: Solveig Gardner Servian
Proofreader: Elaine Leek
Indexer: Silvia Benvenuto
Marketing manager: Alison Borg
Cover design: Jennifer Crisp
Typeset by: C&M Digitals (P) Ltd, Chennai, India
Printed and bound by CPI Group (UK) Ltd,
Croydon, CR0 4YY

Library of Congress Control Number: 2016933356

British Library Cataloguing in Publication data

A catalogue record for this book is available from
the British Library

ISBN 978-1-47398-049-5
ISBN 978-1-47398-050-1 (pbk)

Dear Reader, I hope that whatever your nationality or political persuasion, that you read and think about your present political system and consider how it can be run better and serve and satisfy the interests of more people. Pessimism only makes you depressed and give up. I am forever the optimist, because the one thing that optimism does is make you act. —PK

In admiration of the four Presidents celebrated at Mount Rushmore—George Washington, Thomas Jefferson, Abraham Lincoln, and Theodore Roosevelt.

CONTENTS

ACKNOWLEDGMENTS

I would like to acknowledge, in alphabetical order, the following individuals for their contributions that have helped me in writing this book: William Cotter for his critical reading of my chapter on the Supreme Court; Milton Kotler for his visionary book, *Neighborhood Government*; Nancy Kotler for her critical reading of my manuscript and insistence on balance; Larry Lessig for his powerful writings in *Republic, Lost*; Norman Ornstein for his brilliant observations in *It's Even Worse Than It Looks*; Christian Sarkar for his excellent work on www.fixcapitalism.com and www.democracyindecline.com, and Danny Stern for partnering with me in making this book possible.

ABOUT THE AUTHOR

Philip Kotler is the S. C. Johnson & Son Distinguished Professor of International Marketing at the Kellogg School of Management, Northwestern University. His most recent book, *Confronting Capitalism: Real Solutions for a Troubled Economic System* (2015), calls for both strong economic growth and a better sharing of the gains of economic growth. Professor Kotler is the author of over 50 books on markets and marketing. Trained as an economist at the University of Chicago (under Nobel Laureate, Milton Friedman) and at M.I.T. (under Nobel Laureates, Paul Samuelson and Robert Solow), he has applied his economic knowledge to how markets and marketing works, and was an early developer of modern marketing and the emerging field of behavioral economics. As an expert on how buyers make their buying decisions, he broadened marketing to explain how buyers make their voting decisions on all kinds of issues.

FOREWORD

These are challenging times for democracies. Having barely survived the threat of a Greek exit in 2015, the European Union now faces the possibility of a British exit as well as the greatest refugee crisis since the Second World War. On the other side of the Atlantic, the possible impeachment of Brazilian President Dilma Rousseff on embezzlement charges has led to government paralysis even as the economy confronts a dramatic downturn. Further north, drug trafficking and organized crime threaten to undermine government institutions across Central America. And in the United States, where the legislative process is increasingly characterized by gridlock and polarization, public trust in government has dropped to historic lows. According to a recent survey by the Pew Research Center, only 19 percent of Americans say they trust their government always or most of the time, and nearly 75 percent believe most elected officials put their own interests ahead of the country's.[1] These figures are not likely to improve during the 2016 presidential campaign. As the contours of a vicious general election battle come into focus, the Republican Party is facing an internal struggle over its identity, and record amounts of outside spending are pouring in to influence the results of the election.

How should we measure the health of democracies? This is obviously a complicated question, one that can be answered in various ways but can only be credibly addressed through rigorous analysis independent of politics and ideology. Freedom House, a well-regarded non profit organization that promotes democracy across the globe, attempts to answer the question through its annual *Freedom in the World* report. For the 2016 edition, a team of more than 100 analysts and advisers examined a wide range of issues in 195 countries and 15 territories, and then applied a three-tiered rating system to evaluate the status of their respective political rights and civil liberties. Seventy-two countries registered a drop from the previous year, the largest decline since the beginning of a decade-long slump.[2]

With his new book, *Democracy in Decline*, Philip Kotler brings a fresh perspective to the subject at a moment when new insights are sorely needed. Kotler, the 'father of modern marketing' (as he is affectionately known), has done more than anyone else in his field to revolutionize the theory and practice of marketing. His classic textbook, *Marketing Management*, currently in its fifteenth edition, is essential reading for business students all over the world. By applying rigorous economic analysis and methodology to the discipline, he has elevated what was once an art form (if not an afterthought) into a science – and helped to transform marketing into an indispensable pillar of corporate strategy. One of his core insights is that marketers and consumers are exchanging *values*, not products. The implications of this observation are profound, validated by the fact that today's most successful companies place a higher emphasis on meeting consumers' needs than on maximizing sales. Always attuned to the cultural trends and technological innovations that affect consumer behavior, Kotler has continued to evolve in his thinking over the years. His pioneering work on social marketing, for example, has enabled corporations to embrace social responsibility as a profitable strategy while empowering non profits and public sector professionals to apply corporate marketing strategies as a way to increase social impact.

Most recently, Kotler has turned his eye toward the vulnerabilities in our political and economic systems. In his 2015 book, *Confronting Capitalism*, he explored the key factors undermining economic growth and charted a sustainable path to shared prosperity. Now, with *Democracy in Decline*, he aims to reinvigorate American politics with a set of clear-eyed reforms. Drawing on more than 50 years of research at Northwestern University's Kellogg School of Management, he surveys the American political landscape with the eye of an expert marketing manager and identifies a long-cherished 'product' (democracy) that is no longer satisfying the needs of its 'consumers' (citizens). His diagnoses of the 14 interlocked challenges to U.S. democracy, and his proposals for overcoming each of them, are poised to prompt a robust debate among scholars, practitioners, and engaged citizens. Anyone concerned with the prospects for America's future and democracy around the world would do well to take heed.

Daniel Diermeier, PhD
Dean, Harris School of Public Policy,
The University of Chicago

NOTES

1   www.people-press.org/2015/11/23/beyond-distrust-how-americans-view-their-government/
2   https://freedomhouse.org/report/freedom-world/freedom-world-2016

INTRODUCTION—CHALLENGES TO DEMOCRACY IN A CHANGING WORLD

'It was the best of times, it was the worst of times, it was the age of wisdom, it was the age of foolishness, it was the epoch of belief, it was the epoch of incredulity, it was the season of Light, it was the season of Darkness, it was the spring of hope, it was the winter of despair, we had everything before us, we had nothing before us, we were all going direct to Heaven, we were all going direct the other way.'

Charles Dickens, *A Tale of Two Cities*

The world is changing at a faster rate than ever. Everything is being impacted by globalization, advances in science and technology, and the rise of the Internet and digitalization. The Old World Order is giving way to a New World Order filled with uncertainties and insecurities on the one hand, and accompanied by oceans of new opportunities and possibilities on the other hand.

There are now seven billion people on the Earth, predicted to move to nine billion by 2050. Five billion people live in poverty. Many people of the world are uprooted, moving from the land of their birth to hopefully safer havens. People continue to fight wars. Terrorists are setting off bombs. Many governments repress popular opinion. The cry for popular democracy is everywhere but it is crushed by despots who insist on maintaining order rather than on improving living conditions.

Yes, people need to be governed to avoid anarchy and chaos. But what makes a good government versus an oppressive one? Monarchies are no longer the modern answer. A one political party system as in China is an answer, but people have to pray that it will be benign. Today's major answer is that good government has a better chance if candidates have the right to run for election and if citizens have the right to choose their leaders. Most people today would prefer democracy to autocracy or plutocracy.

But democracy isn't a simple system. It requires more than just running free elections. It requires citizens who are knowledgeable and who show up to vote on Election Day. It requires free assembly of citizens to discuss issues and, when needed, organize a peaceful protest. It requires a free press and two or more political parties who can freely advertise and debate their proposals and their promises.

The United States of America represents such a democracy. It was founded by a set of brilliant individuals who chose to fight for independence from Great Britain and form a new Republic 'of the people, by the people, and for the people.' Thomas Jefferson and the Committee of Five stated in the Declaration of Independence:

> We hold these truths to be self-evident, that all men are created equal, that they are endowed by their Creator with certain unalienable Rights, that among these are *Life, Liberty and the pursuit of Happiness.*

American democracy over the past 240 years has passed through several stages and transformations with great impacts from such Presidents as George Washington, Thomas Jefferson, Andrew Jackson, Abraham Lincoln, Theodore Roosevelt, Franklin Roosevelt, Ronald Reagan, William Clinton, and Barack Obama.

Today there are a large number of new candidates running for President who hope to shape or reshape the nature of U.S. democracy. Seventeen different candidates chose to run for the Republican Party and three candidates chose to run for the Democratic Party. Jeb Bush declared his intention to run for President back in 2013 and others shortly followed. Given that the election would take place in November 2016, these candidates would be running for over 3½ years for this office. It seems that such a long election period is designed not to learn about the candidates' beliefs and values but to see which have sufficient stamina! Each candidate will dedicate most of his or her time, money and energy for 3½ years to speak to crowds and to raise money.

Among the many candidates, two stand out greatly from the other candidates as 'outsiders.' The first 'outsider' is Donald Trump, who commanded the most attention and who is the most outspoken. He defied 'political correctness' by proposing that all illegal Mexicans be sent home and that the U.S. build a wall to be paid for by Mexico to keep further illegal Mexicans out; that Muslims be banned from entering the country; along with other discriminations that run counter to American beliefs and ideals. Yet every new issue in his 'politics of disgust' seems to get him more votes. He attracts mostly low income and angry groups who feel downtrodden, neglected by established politicians and parties, and who want a fresh voice to represent their grievances. Trump is a rare and original phenomenon in American politics who has unnerved everyone in the established conservative Republican Party.

The other 'outsider' is Bernie Sanders, an independent for most of his Senate career, aged 74, and running as a Democratic Socialist. Bernie has eschewed getting funds from billionaires and Super PACs (political action committees, officially known as 'independent expenditure-only committees') and has relied on individual gifts now amounting to multi-millions and averaging $27 a fan. He has developed over 20 carefully crafted liberal proposals along with a cost estimate of each. Among his favorite proposals are free college education, a single payer plan for health coverage, increasing the minimum wage to $15, a higher tax on income and wealth, getting big money out of politics, combating climate change, combating racial prejudice, raising women's rights and gay rights, lowering prescription drug prices, and reforming Wall Street. Underlying his proposals is the idea that an ideal democracy cares about the education, health, and welfare of all of its citizens. His platform has great appeal to young idealistic people and baby boomers who remember the glorious 1960s when they fought for civil rights, gay rights, and women's rights. The major problem for Sanders is whether as President he would have any chance to pass any of his proposals given the gridlocked Congress.

Both the lower income class and the middle class feel marginalized and disempowered. They have anxieties about their jobs and incomes and changing social values. Some candidates readily spin fear and anger messages to get the lower income class to look somewhere else than at the established politicians. Other candidates spin new solutions that are not very feasible. The media is driven by skillful manipulators who aim to exploit existing anxieties, real and perceived.

Whoever becomes the U.S. President will face a dizzying set of unresolved national issues that Congress has refused to act on: Abortion, campaign finance, climate and pollution, consumer protection, drug wars, gun control, healthcare, immigration, infrastructure, military and defense, national debt, poverty, social security and retirement, student loans, and taxes.

Beyond these issues are broader forces and threats that must be understood and managed carefully:

- The Internet and social media have made the world more connected than ever. People around the world have access to more information, more experts, and more rating systems to guide their personal decisions about what and where to buy and who to vote for. The powerful but failed revolutions in Egypt, Syria, and Libya were made possible by the Internet's ability to connect people. On the negative side, people are becoming more tribal and reading and listening more to their own groups and paying less attention to other voices. Everyone is camping in his or her own comfortable bubble of information and not seeing other points of view.

- Advances in science and technology are changing people's views about the nature of the cosmos. We hear more about living in a universe (or multiverses) with billions of stars and planets that is expanding at an accelerating rate, all raising the question of who we are and what life means.

- More productive work is being done by robots and artificial intelligent apps that threaten whether there will be enough jobs to provide employment for the world's growing population. Many Americans are worried about the future and ready to blame the Washington establishment, or Wall Street, or minority groups, or foreigners.

- There is increased concern about slower economic growth. China formerly fueled the growth of many nations by its endless need for so much food, minerals, and products from other nations who in turn benefitted from cheaper Chinese products. But China is slowing down and facing major financial problems coming from expanding too fast. Most nations today are encumbered by high debt and without the ability to raise enough tax revenue to maintain their physical, education, and health infrastructure.

- The world is marked by a growing concentration of wealth where the top 1% may earn or own more than 30, 40 or 50% of that nation's income or wealth. For the U.S., this means that concentrated wealth runs Congress, not the people, and Congress members have no incentive to vote for a better system.

- The world also has rogue nations that threaten the lives of other people. North Korea keeps building atomic bombs. Iran has only recently agreed to stop building their own atomic bombs. Russia under Putin invaded and annexed Crimea which belonged to Ukraine. An extreme movement of Jihadist Muslims created ISIS (sometimes called ISIL or Daesh) and captured territory in the Middle East where it trains terrorists and suicide bombers and destroys holy treasures of other cultures.

Clearly, the next American President will face an insurmountable number of problems. A Republican President would probably focus on terror and foreign policy. A Democratic President would focus on jobs and the economy. Both would be simplifying the challenges. One can only hope that the next President can build an alliance with other nations who care about freedom and democracy and who will work together to meet these challenges. These problems will continue past the next few Presidents but we hope that the wisdom is there to take the right actions at the right times.

The next U.S. President has to worry about a number of domestic issues that affect the performance of democracy itself. There are not enough informed citizens and there are not enough citizens who vote. We are witnessing efforts to increase the gerrymandering of Congressional districts so that incumbents can remain in power indefinitely. We are witnessing violations of the Voting Rights Act of 1965 and finding state legislatures requiring more tangible proofs of citizenship that fall hard on poorer citizens. We are seeing a gridlocked Congress with House Representatives ready to shut down government over abortion and gun ownership issues. We see a Supreme Court that decided on a 5 to 4 vote in the *Citizens United v. Federal Electoral Commission (FEC)* case that corporations are people and have the right to spend almost unlimited money backing preferred candidates. We have to worry that elections are growing costlier and that each candidate and elected official has to spend more time in fund raising than in reviewing legislative issues. Big money is electing our politicians and using lobbying to influence their votes. We also need to consider term limits, which were placed on the U.S. President to serve no more than two terms, and possibly should be applied to Congress members and Supreme Court justices. And there are many other issues.

As an economist, I published *Confronting Capitalism: Real Solutions for a Troubled Economic System* in 2015. I identified 14 shortcomings plaguing American Capitalism. It is true that American Capitalism has created great economic wealth. But until the Affordable Care Act was enacted in 2010, 45 million Americans were without health insurance. Today 15% of the American public are living in deep poverty. Many Americans are working for only $7.45 an hour and require food stamps to have enough to eat. The real wages of most American workers are lower in their real buying power than they were back in 1970. Most college graduates are carrying high college debt, preventing them from buying major products and starting families. We won't mention our decaying infrastructure, our huge and growing federal debt, the Occupy Wall Street movement, and other problems. Many are alarmed about these problems in the belief that many solutions are available for fixing these problems.

In this new book, *Democracy in Decline*, I want to examine how well democracy is serving voters. As a professional economist and marketer, I am used to evaluating products. If we look at democracy as a product, we would ask how well the product is made, how much it is satisfying its consumers, how well it is being sold. Judging from the widespread anger and disappointment expressed by countless citizens during the 2016 elections, democracy is not fully fulfilling the expectations of citizens. They see and hear many candidates promising many different things and taking so much time in broadcast and print media to promote their positions that we hardly hear any other news during this period. There must be a better way to find good candidates, learn their messages and positions, and judge who to vote for. I know when a product is working and its method of selling is working. I believe that there are some design flaws in the present system that can be corrected. We can design a better performing democratic system.

There was a time when local citizens got together to decide on the issues facing their community. Small towns in Vermont and New Hampshire would run several well-attended citizen meetings a year and decide on community issues by a majority vote on each issue. This was a time when We the People, not We the Corporations, ran the country.

Today there is a Congressional election every two years. Fewer than 60% of eligible voters vote in a presidential election. Over 96% of politicians are likely to stay in office. Politicians desperately need money to run their campaigns. Several of them get their money from billionaires or multi-millionaires. They can't get this money without owing something to their donors. The result: Much legislation is conservative, not only to protect big fortunes but also to enlarge them. We have rapidly moved from being a democracy into an oligarchy or a plutocracy.

My conclusion is that the weakening of democracy is reducing the Capitalist system's ability to produce benefits for the majority of our people. Democracy is increasingly serving the narrow interest of the wealthy.

FOURTEEN SHORTCOMINGS OF DEMOCRACY

1   Low voter literacy, turnout, and engagement.
2   Shortage of highly qualified and visionary candidates.
3   Blind belief in American exceptionalism.
4   Growing public antipathy toward government.
5   Two-party gridlock preventing needed legislation.
6   Growing role of money in politics.
7   Gerrymandering empowering incumbents to get re-elected forever.
8   Caucuses and primaries leading candidates to adopt more extreme positions.
9   Continuous conflict between the President and Congress.
10 Continuous conflict between the federal and state governments.
11 The Supreme Court's readiness to revise legislative actions.
12 The difficulty of passing new amendments.
13 The difficulty of developing a sound foreign policy.
14 Making government agencies more accountable.

I will examine these 14 challenges to American democracy. Most Americans haven't taken a course in civics or they forgot how the system is supposed to work. I aim to deliver a better understanding of how government works in practice.

American politicians always laud American exceptionalism. They boast that America has the best economic system (capitalism), and the best political system (democracy). Having become the richest nation in the world, Americans may look like the Chosen People. We are pointed to the specialness of the U.S. Constitution and the genius of the founding fathers—Benjamin Franklin, James Madison, Thomas Jefferson, John Adams, and many others. This gifted group hammered together a Constitution and a Bill of Rights that promised to deliver to Americans a better 'life, liberty, and the pursuit of happiness.'

Now let's be clear, the Constitution and Bill of Rights have been wonderful! Citizens are free to start any business and succeed or fail to the extent that their products and services satisfy their customers. Businesses are not run by the government but by private citizens who go solo or partner or incorporate to form organizations to carry on their commerce. In fact, the view is that government should be minimal: it should provide defense, roads, police and firemen, harbors and bridges, education and health facilities, and justice for all.

Democracy is based on the notion that the people should shape a nation's future. My aim is to describe how we can meet the 14 challenges through improving the workings of democracy's major political institutions—Congress, the President, the Supreme Court, the two Political Parties, the States, and Government Agencies.

I believe that reforms are necessary and possible. We are quickly losing representative government as voter registration is restrained, as redistricting is leading to gerrymandered districts, and as campaign finance is now in the hands of millionaires and billionaires. I am writing as a Ph.D. economist and an interested voting citizen. I am aware of how complex our democratic system is. Hopefully, in trying to untangle the web of problems in our democracy, my concerns and proposed solutions will help citizens who have wondered about the same issues. I hope that my observations and findings generate discussion, debate, and decision making.

In the year 2000, Colin Crouch published a new book with the title *Coping with Post-Democracy*. He defined post-democracy as a system that has the trappings of democracy—free speech, elections—but has become more limited in delivering real democracy. People vote but it doesn't make a difference. The political system has serious problems but it has not evolved to the point where it can deliver real solutions. The problem is that the system is no longer controlled by the voters but by the rich and superrich. We don't want to settle for a post-democracy. This book is about getting back to a real democracy.

CHAPTER 1

WHY DEMOCRACY ISN'T WORKING WELL IN AMERICA OR ELSEWHERE—WHY HAVING ELECTIONS ISN'T ENOUGH

'People shouldn't be afraid of their government. Governments should be afraid of their people.'

Alan Moore, *V for Vendetta*

W e live in an age when the majority of people say they want to live in a democracy. But still, many of the world's seven billion people are suffering from oppression, corruption, and dictatorship. They have a terribly low living standard and they don't feel safe or free to talk. They yearn for democracy and prosperity. We saw them start a freedom movement in Egypt on January 25, 2011. Even earlier, on December 10, 2010, demonstrations started in Tunisia precipitated by the high unemployment, food inflation, corruption, poor living conditions, and a lack of political freedom. The Egyptian and Tunisian revolutions then led to demonstrations in other Arab countries, including Yemen, Bahrain, Jordan, Syria, and Libya.

More recently the dictatorial regime and war in Syria has led more than four million refugees to leave Syria for Europe and other destinations where they could acquire a modicum of peace and opportunity. Their hearts beat for a place where their families can live normal lives and find work and freedom. Democracy is the system they yearn for and Europe and America come first in their minds.

America's experience with democracy began in 1776 with the start of the American Revolution when the American colonies broke away from Britain. The Continental Congress worked to design a new political system, a democracy. Some elements were drawn from the ancient Greek idea of democracy as practiced in Athens, where eligible citizens listened to orators and directly voted on various proposals to improve their lives and living standards. More than

2,000 years later, in early New England towns, citizens would meet to vote on various proposals affecting their community.

On July 4, 1786, the U.S. founders drafted and passed the Declaration of Independence that stated that men are endowed by their Creator with unalienable Rights to 'Life, Liberty and the pursuit of Happiness.' Almost a year later, on May 25, 1787, they met in the Pennsylvania State House (now Independence Hall) in Philadelphia to begin to draft a Constitution to replace the Articles of Confederation. They ended their work and adopted and signed the Constitution on September 17, 1787. The process of ratifying the Constitution began that day, and ended when the state of Rhode Island ratified it on May 29, 1790, three years later.

Then on December 15, 1791, the Congress added The Bill of Rights to the Constitution as the first ten amendments establishing freedom of speech, freedom of the press, freedom of assembly, and the right to a fair and speedy trial. They were greatly influenced by the July 14, 1789 storming of the Bastille fortress and by the French Revolution dissolving the French Monarchy and replacing it with a system that would deliver to the people 'liberty, equality, and fraternity.' Many of us would prefer not to live than live without the values these words represent. The French Revolution was greatly influenced by our Declaration of Independence, and in turn influenced our passage of the Bill of Rights.

Two hundred years later, in May 1989, a million Chinese crowded into Tiananmen Square in central Beijing to call for greater democracy and to do away with the one-party rule of the Chinese Communist Party. The protesters kept up daily vigils for three weeks and on June 4, 1989, Chinese troops and security police stormed the Square and fired indiscriminately into the crowds. Many young students fled; others stoned the attacking troops and set fire to military vehicles. At least 300 protestors were killed and as many as 10,000 were arrested.

On March 19, 2003, the U.S. Government invaded Iraq on the grounds that the Saddam Hussein Government possessed weapons of mass destruction and that this posed a terror threat to peace-loving countries. Although no such weapons were found, George W. Bush in a speech to the World Affairs Council of Philadelphia on December 12, 2005, justified the invasion as our effort to help the Iraqis build democratic institutions such as a rule of law, freedom of speech, freedom of assembly, a free economy, and freedom to worship. In retrospect, implanting democracy in a desert country appears a naïve aspiration and more a cover to disguise the real reason for the invasion, namely to protect our need for oil from the Middle East.

On August 8, 2013, public commemorations took place in Myanmar (Burma) to mark the 25th anniversary of uprisings that launched their pro-democracy movement. For over 20 years, Aung San Suu Kyi was kept under house arrest by the military to prevent her in leading a pro-democracy movement. After her release, she stirred up the pro-democracy movement. In November 2015, her party, the National League for Democracy, or NLD, won more than 80% of the contested parliamentary seats. Aung San is now the most important person in Myanmar and she is announcing new policies to build a better life for more people.

Why do I mention these episodes? They show the power and passion for the idea of democracy in different parts of the world. Is democracy the right system for every country in the world? No, not every country is ready for democracy. But when enough people believe in the idea of freedom and popular voting, such a country is ready for democracy.

WHAT QUALIFIES A COUNTRY AS BEING A DEMOCRACY?

There are probably more countries claiming to be a democracy than the actual number of democracies. In one study, the following 73 countries were listed as democracies:

> Argentina, Australia, Austria, Belgium, Benin, Brazil, Bulgaria, Canada, Cape Verde, Chile, Croatia, Cyprus, Czech Republic, Denmark, Dominican Republic, El Salvador, Estonia, Finland, France, Georgia, Germany, Ghana, Greece, Honduras, Hungary, Iceland, India, Indonesia, Ireland, Israel, Italy, Japan, Jamaica, Kiribati, North Korea, South Korea, Latvia, Estonia, Lithuania, Mali, Malta, Mexico, Micronesia, Mongolia, Namibia, the Netherlands, New Zealand, Nicaragua, Norway, Palau, Peru, Philippines, Poland, Portugal, Romania, Singapore, Slovakia, Slovenia, South Africa, South Korea, Spain, Suriname, Sweden, Thailand, Taiwan, Tonga, Trinidad and Tobago, Tuvalu, Ukraine, United Kingdom, United States of America, Uruguay.[1]

One needs to be suspicious of some of the countries included in this list. How did North Korea get on this list? Maybe these countries run elections, however honest or dishonest they are. But it should be noted that Russia is not on this list and yet it has elections.

The Economist Intelligence Unit (EIU) prepared a much better analysis of democracy. The EIU measures the extent of democracy in 167 countries based on 60 indicators grouped in five different categories measuring pluralism, civil liberties, and political culture.[2] The EIU categorized these 167 countries into four regime types: *Full democracies, flawed democracies, hybrid regimes,* and *authoritarian regimes.* Only 24 countries were identified as full democracies and they covered 12.5% of the world's population. Flawed democracies numbered 52 countries which covered 35.5% of the world's population. Full and flawed democracies operate in about 76 countries of the world.

Freedom House is another source of measures on how many democracies there are and it distinguishes between free and partly free democracies.[3] Their discouraging finding is that the world is experiencing an eight-year decline in political rights and civil liberties. They saw an abridgement of freedom and democracy in such countries as Egypt, Russia, Ukraine, Azerbaijan, Turkey, and Venezuela. Their governments have either been taken over by military coups or authoritarian leaders bent on destroying the opposition and perpetuating their power and oppression.

Unfortunately, many democracies around the world function poorly. Democracies in Latin America have to contend with a high level of poverty, high income inequality, and rampant corruption. In Brazil, the executive branch and legislative branch have difficulty getting broad agreement given that there are 13 political parties. President Rousseff has to build continuous coalitions to get anything done. She created at great cost a cabinet of 39 ministries to please the various parties. Raising political money has led to a major corruption scandal involving Petrobras, the large oil company. Much has to be done to clean up democracy in many of the world's democracies.[4]

WHAT IS DEMOCRACY ANYWAY?

Democracy comes from the Greek words 'demos' (people) and 'krates' (rule), which literally means 'people power.' Democracy is essentially a political system where the ultimate power lies with the people. It lies in their power to vote for or against particular laws, rules, and regulations, and the freely rendered majority opinion determines the outcome. The seed idea of democracy is self-government and majority rule.

Intrinsic to democracy is the idea of one person, one vote! If one person can cast more votes than another person, the system of democracy is corrupted. Consider this. In a monarchy, only one person can vote, namely the King. Everyone else's vote is irrelevant. In an aristocracy, the aristocrats have more voting power than the plebeians, even though there are far fewer aristocrats than ordinary citizens. In a plutocracy, the rich have much more voting power than the average citizens. This can happen if the rich use their money to influence the media to influence average citizens to favor certain candidates over others. The Koch brothers are plutocrats in that they have declared that they are ready to spend almost a billion dollars to get their favorite conservative candidates elected. They have a whole plan to infiltrate American state and city legislatures with legislators who will represent their ultra-conservative views. Sheldon Adelson, another plutocrat, is unrestrained in spending his money to get conservative politicians elected.

The source of this voting corruption of democracy lies in the lack of restrictions on campaign finance.[5] The big setback was the decision of the Supreme Court in the *Citizens United* case that recognized companies as 'persons' who could spend unlimited amounts on political campaigns and candidates: 'Hostile forces in Congress, the U.S. Supreme Court and state legislatures are rolling back decades' worth of progress on campaign finance reform.'[6]

Clearly, democracy has some design flaws. But as Winston Churchill famously said, 'Democracy is the worst form of government, except for all the other forms that have been tried from time to time.' It is the only political system with moral legitimacy. Its major virtue is that it has the capacity to be 'self-correcting.' Inept leaders and policies can be replaced.

MOST DEMOCRACIES ARE REPRESENTATIVE DEMOCRACIES, NOT DIRECT DEMOCRACIES

A *direct democracy* exists when citizens gather in (say) a small New England community to discuss and cast their votes on various local issues with the majority vote winning. The community would run meetings usually attended by all citizens. This was a frequent feature in the early Colonial and post-Colonial days of the U.S. Today it takes place notably in California where many referendums are proposed by citizens and citizens have a chance to vote on them.

But in larger, more populous areas where there are many issues, it is more expedient for the citizens to elect a set of representatives to vote on the issues for the citizens. This is variously called an *indirect democracy*, a *representative democracy*, or *a republic*. In fact, the U.S. is more a Republic than a Democracy in its original sense. The citizens may not have the time or aptitude to study and vote on the various issues. They elect candidates they trust to study the issues and vote for their interests. The framers of our Constitution shared a fear of direct elections. Elbridge Gerry of the Massachusetts delegation said: 'The evils we experience flow from the excess of democracy.' Fellow delegate Virginia Governor Edmund Randolph said: 'The people do not want [lack] virtue, but are the dupes of pretended patriots. In tracing these evils to their origin every man had found it in the turbulence and follies of democracy.'

The framers knew that indirect elections—voters electing representatives who voted on issues—was the key to overcoming this problem. The citizens would vote to choose among the candidates who were running for office, rather than on the issues themselves. Still, citizens retain the ultimate control because they have the opportunity every two years to re-vote on the representatives they want. They will vote to replace disappointing representatives with new representatives who come closer to matching their issue preferences.

This system of representative democracy raises an interesting question on where these representatives owe their interest. Consider a bill that proposes expanding this year's military budget by 10%. A representative needs to decide in whose interest he or she should vote. There are three possibilities:

1   The representative can vote for what he or she perceives to be the majority opinion in the district.
2   Or vote for what he or she thinks is in the best interest of the country.
3   Or vote for what his or her party favors.

Many observers side with (1), that the representative should reflect the majority opinion in the district. That's why the district voted for the representative. If the representative consistently votes differently, he or she will be voted out of office.

Other observers want the representative to be a statesman. What is best for the nation? The representative may feel that the country's military budget is big enough and vote against increasing the military budget.

Still others who are more cynical will expect the representative to vote for what is in the representative's best interest. If the party pressures the representative to vote for a 10% increase in the military budget, the representative will vote for it. Every representative needs to get re-elected and it is the party that will help him or her with the finances to get re-elected. This third way of voting is probably the most frequent. It explains the lack of statesmen among our politicians.

The critic Michael Moore thinks that American citizens have lost the right to vote for what the majority favors. A poll might show that 80% of citizens want the Affordable Care Act (ACA) of 2010. But under our system, some active

House Representatives may keep attacking and emasculating the ACA until it no longer works or collapses.

The Idea of a Representative Democracy Evolved Over Time

Wherever people live together, they need to have political organization. They need to decide how much liberty and how much authority to accept. At one extreme, people can have extreme liberty—minimal government—but this might lead to anarchy and the survival of the strongest. At the other extreme, the people might accept a supreme leader or a dictator where individual interests are submerged. At what point must individual rights be curbed to produce the greatest good for the greatest number of people? The public and the government must determine what the proper relationship is between the state and its citizens.

Political theory started with Plato and Aristotle in ancient Greece. Plato had the view that a good government would promulgate an austere code in diet, dress, and amusements. Plato did not favor universal suffrage and believed that only capable and informed citizens should have a right to vote.

Aristotle (384–322 B.C.) wrote insightfully and systematically on the different political systems. The Romans contributed greatly to the literature on how to run a parliamentary system under the rule of law. During the Dark Ages, most European populations were ruled by kings and tribal leaders. The King was seen to have the right to rule through God, not through the consent of the governed. Kings varied in their views on how to use their power.

Niccolò Machiavelli (1469–1527), the first deep political thinker since Aristotle, became famous for advising kings on how to treat their subjects in his book, *The Prince*. As the founder of modern political science, Machiavelli focused on the art of government rather than on developing a theory of the state. He considered such questions as whether a Prince should be liberal or mean, whether he should be loved or feared, and whether he should keep promises or not. He concluded that the Prince should seek to be seen as liberal but have a reputation for meanness. He would be more effective if he is feared than loved. Machiavelli drew a picture of people as fickle, false, and covetous and the Prince should deal with a strong hand.

In the 16th Century, the Protestant revolt took place to challenge the Catholic Church and its Popes. **Martin Luther** (1483–1546), **John Calvin** (1509–1564),

(Continued)

(Continued)

and other religious leaders placed their faith in reading the Bible rather than in the pronouncements of the Pope. The doctrine arose that people could resist tyranny, not by the masses rebelling, but by the efforts of their magistrates or assemblies.

In the 17th Century, new rumblings occurred about democratic ideas. Political thinkers considered the concept of liberty, the nature of popular consent, the social contract as a basis for the state, and the right of revolution against an oppressive government. **John Milton** (1608–1674) wrote about the freedom of the press. He viewed rulers as the agent of the people. He said that their power should be limited by laws and that the people are sovereign and liberty is their birthright. People should have a wide sphere of activity unrestricted by government. They should have the opportunity to work out their own destiny in their own way.

Thomas Hobbes (1588–1679) held a different view in *Leviathan*. He favored divine authority because he viewed men as bestial in a state of nature and they needed a common power to overawe and control them into keeping their agreements. He favored a ruler with absolute power and people should surrender all their rights to the sovereign.

John Locke (1632–1704), in *Two Treatises of Government*, embraced a liberal view. He attacked the idea of a divine prerogative and even justified the right of revolution against an oppressive government. He developed a systematic discussion of the origin, character, and scope of government. He said that the laws of nature indicate the rules for the conduct of men. Men must receive equal treatment under the law. They have the natural rights to life, liberty, and property. They form a contract whose purpose is to preserve and protect these inalienable rights. Government was the agency of the collective will and it could be called to account if it oversteps. Locke favored majority rule and the separation of powers. He maintained, however, that the legislative branch of government should rule supreme.

Baron de Montesquieu (1689–1755) wrote *The Spirit of Laws* in 1748, advocating the principle of separation of government powers into legislative, executive, and judicial to preserve the equilibrium of government. He warned against any two branches of government being under the same leadership.

Jean-Jacques Rousseau (1712–1778), in *Of the Social Contract, Principles of Political Right*, held a natural view of man, who he sees as coming together to form a social contract. He held that men could revoke the social contract if it was oppressing their natural rights. He held that the right of revolution was an inalienable right. In many ways, he was the apostle of the French Revolution and his writings led to the French Declaration of the Rights of Man.

These Ideas Come to America

So many of the previous ideas came to America and fortified the idea of declaring independence from Britain and shaping a new political system and Constitution. **Thomas Paine** (1737–1809) in *Common Sense* popularized the idea of popular sovereignty and the right of revolution. Locke's ideas greatly influenced Thomas Jefferson, who was the main author of the Constitution. **Thomas Jefferson** (1743–1826) held that the role of government is to guarantee the rights of citizens and the consent of the governed. He wanted citizens to have the right to criticize government and those who govern. He believed in:

1   Equal and exact justice.
2   Rights of election.
3   Majority rule.
4   Guarantee of civil liberties.
5   Subordination of military to civil authority.
6   Economical administration.

He believed in the importance of local government. He also believed in the periodic revision of the Constitution to meet the changing conditions in the world. He believed in the separation of Church and State.

Jefferson's nemesis was **John Adams** (1735–1826), who died the same year as Jefferson. Adams distrusted the masses and defended inequality among men and advocated a government by an aristocracy based on birth, education, and wealth.

A more populist view of American government finally came with the election of **Andrew Jackson** (1767–1845). Jackson extended suffrage, abolished property and religious qualifications for holding office, aimed his appeal mostly at the voters rather than the party officials, and favored popular ratification of state constitutions.

John Stuart Mill (1806–1873), although British, contributed important ideas about a democratic society. He wanted a nation to be 'a free marketplace for ideas.' He valued freedom and said that people should be free to say and think what they want. Citizens should pick the rulers and not let the few tell the many what to do.

(Continued)

(Continued)

All said, the past two centuries have shown notable progress in human rights and political organization. Political privileges of birth and class have tended to disappear. The rule of law has grown stronger governing personal rights as defined by the Bill of Rights. The U.S. Constitution remains strong as the ultimate document defining American democracy.

WHAT ARE THE MAJOR BENEFITS CLAIMED FOR A REPRESENTATIVE DEMOCRACY?

The first major benefit is the maximization of individual liberty. This includes the freedoms of association, speech, voting, and uncensored media access in addition to other basic human rights. The U.N. Commission on Human Rights stated that no society without basic civil liberties can be classified as a democracy. It is essential that people can express their views and enjoy assemblage and debates to build consensus.

The second major benefit is that all citizens have legal rights to a speedy trial and an impartial judge and jury. They are given an opportunity to defend themselves and if convicted, they will not be subject to torture or inhumane treatment.

The third benefit is that a democracy is likely to experience less internal violence, fewer wars, and less mass murder by governments. This leads to more stability and gives the citizens a chance to change their representatives with peaceful means rather than through violence.

Clearly, the first sign of moving to a more authoritarian regime is that the leader or party starts abridging civil liberties of freedom to assemble or speak or vote or have access to media conveying many opinions about nation events and government decisions.

Fortunately, the U.S. still operates as a full democracy with its civil liberties intact. The U.S. has been in the forefront of advocating the spread of democracy, but with limited success. It tried to create democratic governments in Iraq and Afghanistan after its military intervention only to realize how tribal these countries are and their lack of readiness for full democracy. Some might even argue that countries such as these would achieve faster economic growth under a benign authoritarian regime than under a gridlocked democratic system. Look at China's 15 years of rapid economic growth and astonishing reduction of poverty under a Communist one-party system. Contrast this to India's slower rate of growth under the regime of a democratic political system. Needless to say, the U.S. accepts the authoritarian systems of many of its allies in the Middle East because economic self-interest takes priority over spreading democracy to countries that are not ready for it.

WHAT IS THE DIFFERENCE BETWEEN A PRESIDENTIAL SYSTEM AND A PARLIAMENTARY SYSTEM?

The U.S. representative democracy is called a presidential system where every four years the citizens cast their vote for the President. The U.S. consists of a two-party system where each party proposes a candidate. Citizens choose between the two opposing party candidates, the winner being the one who receives the most electoral votes (this is not necessarily the popular vote, to be explained later). The new President can run again four years later but cannot serve more than two full terms.

The citizens also vote for their Representatives and Senators. Many will be elected from a different party than the President's party. This leads to a check and balance system where the President and the Congress can be at odds. The U.S. has a bicameral legislature with each state allowed to vote for a number of House Representatives that will reflect the State's size and a Senator who might be up for election or re-election. Today the U.S. House of Representatives has 435 members and the U.S. Senate has 100 Senators, given that there are 50 states and each is entitled to two Senators.

The national elections take place every two years. In the past, campaigning activity would usually start up about six months before the election. At least there would be 18 months of no electioneering. Today we have permanent campaigning. As soon as House Members are elected, they have to think of lining up supporters and donors who will finance their campaign for re-election in two years. It is estimated that a House Member might spend as much as one-third of his or her time raising money and making friends. At least Senators who are elected for six years are free from active campaigning for re-election for a much longer time.

Today's candidates are guided by marketing and public relations (PR) people and consultants. They need to become a brand. They cannot let any opposition members look good. The Republican Mitch McConnell said just after Barack

Obama won in 2008, 'our number one goal is to make Barack Obama a one-term President.'

The cost of campaigning in the U.S. presidential system keeps growing. The 2016 cost estimate is that politicians and political groups will spend between $7–$10 billion on this election. Billionaires Charles and David Koch plan to spend almost $1 billion to influence the election. This is the highest cost yet in carrying on a U.S. presidential election. Much of the higher cost is due to the Supreme Court's 5 to 4 *Citizens United v. Federal Election Commission* decision in 2010, recognizing a company as a person and opening up floodgates of money to go to PACs and Super PACs. In addition, this election attracted more presidential candidates and many more billionaires to fund their preferred candidates.

What is a PAC and a Super PAC?

A PAC is a federal political action committee that raises money to defeat or elect candidates (Senators, Representatives, Presidents) to federal office. PACs must register with the Federal Election Commission. PACs may receive up to $5,000 from an individual, another PAC or party committee each calendar year. PACs can give $5,000 to a candidate committee per election cycle (primary, general, or special). They can also give up to $15,000 each year to any national party committee and up to $5,000 annually to any other PAC. Corporations, unions, and associations cannot make direct contributions or expenditures in connection with any federal election. However, they may set up PACs that 'can only solicit contributions from individuals associated with sponsoring organization.' Examples include a Microsoft PAC, a Teamsters PAC, or a National Rifle Association PAC. PACs have been influencing elections and campaigns since they first appeared in 1943.

Citizens can contribute money directly to parties and candidates as well. Individuals can give a maximum of $30,800 to a national political party committee such as the Republican National Committee and to an individual candidate in the amount of $2,500 per election.

Super PACs first emerged as a result of the Supreme Court's 5–4 *Citizens United* decision in January 2010. The Court defined corporations as persons that have the right to free speech. It gave corporations and unions the right to raise unlimited sums of money from corporations, unions, and associations and to spend unlimited sums for or against political candidates. However, Super PACs are prohibited from donating money directly to political candidates. They cannot coordinate their efforts with campaigns or political parties. Super PACs are required to report their donors to the Federal Election Commission on a monthly or semiannual basis.

Technically, Super PACs must be 'operated exclusively to promote social welfare.' Political activity is allowed but must not be the organization's 'primary' mission. Yet the current Inland Revenue Services (IRS) commissioner said that groups could spend up to 49% of revenues on political activity and still keep their tax exemption.

As of February 1, 2016, 2,186 groups organized as Super PACs have reported total receipts of $353,533,929 and total independent expenditures of $140,079,965 in the 2016 cycle.

Presidential systems are found in at least 48 countries of the world, with many variations. One of the features of a presidential system is that the voters can never unelect the whole government with one stroke.

Let's turn to parliamentary systems. These systems can unelect the whole government with one stroke. Parliamentary systems are found in 60 countries, including all the British colonies and many countries in Europe and elsewhere.[7] In a parliamentary system, the voters vote for a party more than a person. When a party wins, it appoints its leader who is called the Prime Minister. The Prime Minister can be removed by legislators in a vote of no confidence. Or the voters can elect a different party at the next election.

The parliamentary system first developed in England in the 1700s. It consisted of a House of Commons and a House of Lords. Today in the U.K. there are two major parties — the Conservatives and Labour — and several smaller parties. At an election, one party will receive the majority of votes and form the government. The head of the winning party becomes the Prime Minister. The Prime Minister and the party appoint the other ministers. The party remains in power until either a re-election date is set or there is a no-confidence vote in Parliament. In the latter case, the party has to schedule an election to take place at a certain date, and the campaigning of the parties can begin. Usually campaigning will last for 30 days and the winning party takes over.

There are at least three alleged benefits with a parliamentary system:

1   Elections can be called outside of the normal schedule when Parliament reports a no-confidence vote in the majority party.
2   The majority party can get new legislation passed faster and easier than in the 'grid-locked' presidential system.
3   The majority party is more flexible about shifting course sensing the pressure of the voters.

My conclusion is that the U.S. needs some of the elements of a parliamentary system so that if a great proportion of voters feel that the country is going nowhere and want to consider throwing out the present ruling party and starting fresh, it would have a chance to do this. Under the present presidential system, a great number of legislators continue running the country whoever wins the presidency. There is no chance to throw everyone out and start afresh! We need to realize that there is no chance to move to a parliamentary system without changing the U.S. Constitution.

In a sense, our framers wanted the power in the system to be fragmented. The original founders were largely rich people: Landowners, manufacturers, merchants, shipbuilders, and bankers. They wanted to create the semblance of democracy but without giving too much power to the masses. Slaves and women couldn't vote. The framers favored a republic to a democracy. In fact, the word 'democracy' isn't mentioned in the Declaration of Independence nor in the Constitution. Control and legislation would largely be in the hands of Representatives who are more likely to protect the interests of the wealthier propertied class. Although Representatives and Senators would be elected by popular vote, the Supreme Court would not be subject to popular vote.

Checks and balances were built into the system to prevent legislation being carried too far by the popular vote. The framers, while not wanting a monarchy because of their terrible experience with Britain, still wanted a country ruled by meritorious people rather than just a popular vote. Even as a representative democracy, voting periods cannot bring about a whole new group of leaders. The President is voted on every four years, one-third of the Senate is voted on every two years, all of the House of Representatives are voted on every two years, and the judiciary is appointed for life.

Even Senators were originally to be appointed by the state legislatures, not directly by the voters. Finally, in 1913, the 17th Amendment was passed turning over the election of Senators to the voters in each state.

IT IS NOT ENOUGH FOR A COUNTRY TO RUN ELECTIONS

Let's establish that running elections would be one sign that a country might be a democracy. But let's add some additional conditions:

- Every citizen can vote.
- Citizens can assemble and are free to speak and exchange views, including the chance to organize a peaceful protest.

- The country has a free press so that newspapers, radio and TV, and digital media are free to report news and opinions.
- Citizens are free to have any religious beliefs they choose.
- Citizens are free to start businesses or choose the businesses they want to work in if jobs are available.

Each condition is subject to further qualifying. Consider 'every citizen can vote.' In a real democracy, it would be one citizen, one vote. There would be no stuffing of ballot boxes with false names or the names of deceased people. There would be no one paying money on the side to voters if they voted for a certain candidate. There would be no threatening-looking persons hanging around polling booths who look like they would harm you if you didn't vote in the right way. There would not be very short hours for casting a vote, or voting centers that are far and difficult to reach.

Consider 'freedom of assembly.' Can the government stop certain groups from assembling because they have radical ideas, or form gangs, or carry a lot of guns? Can the government put a limit on how many people can gather to protest a certain issue?

Consider 'freedom of the press.' Are the press members sufficiently diverse in their opinions so that citizens hear a range of views? Is the press permitted to say bad things about the country's president or his or her political party? How should the country handle press members who distort the truth or even lie in quoting their findings? One of today's major issues is to protect the Internet's 'net neutrality.' Internet service providers such as Big Cable and Big Telecom wanted to slow down websites they dislike or disagree with in the interests of giving faster access time to businesses over citizens. Fortunately, the FCC proposed new rules protecting net neutrality for years to come.

Consider 'freedom of religion.' Are people relatively free to change their religious affiliation or even to decide to be an agnostic or atheist? Does any religious group have considerable power to influence legislation in their favor?

Finally, consider 'freedom to start a business or join a business.' Are citizens free to move to other cities in search of a best job? Are they free to choose the work they want to do, including starting their own business if they can find the capital?

WHAT DO MOST PEOPLE WANT FROM THEIR SOCIETY?

What constitutes a good society? This question would come up if a group has gathered to design a new society or a utopia. The agreement would be high on the following items:

- We would want to have a good chance for decent and safe food, clothing, and shelter.
- We would hope to have good health care and facilities.
- We would hope to benefit from a good educational system.
- We would want to be able to gather with others and speak freely.
- We would be free to worship where and how we wish.
- We would want free and honest reporting of news and opinion.
- We would want good opportunities for entertainment and safe travel.
- We would want a government that works well, gets things done, and is trying to improve life for all of us.

WHAT WOULD CITIZENS WANT FROM THEIR POLITICAL INSTITUTIONS?

What would citizens want to see in their political institutions? If we polled citizens about the features they would want in their political institutions, the following would draw high agreement:

- We want to have regular elections where we can express whether we are satisfied with the President and his party and individual legislators.
- We want the election period to be short and without much money being spent by the candidates to influence voting or to slur opponents and we would not want powerful groups to spend excessive amounts of money to influence or buy votes.
- We would prefer that political candidates get their campaign money from the government rather than raising funds without limit from wealthy donors.
- We want affairs to be settled by the rule of law and the existence of legal precedents.
- We want Congress and the Courts to respect property rights and human rights.
- We want a Congress that is able to pass needed laws efficiently and fairly.
- We want a government where the Executive branch respects the Legislative branch and the reverse is true.
- We want an efficient and fair court system where each case is decided quickly on its merits and not on one ideology or another.
- We want a government that respects our right to privacy while balancing it with our needs for security.
- We want a federal government that respects states' rights but also states that are willing to work with other states to get some uniformity in our laws.
- We want a federal government that defines a thoughtful foreign policy and aids industry in growing their foreign business.
- We want a federal government that builds national strength and a high level of national security.

The U.S. needs to recognize how far it is from obtaining these simple wished-for arrangements. There is a two-party system sworn to two opposite ideologies and not willing to work with each other and seek compromises. There is great tension between the White House and Congress, stunting the President's ability to lead. The Supreme Court is ideologically divided, where many of the nine votes are predictable whatever the case to be a 5-to-4 decision. The electioneering period runs much too long and is too expensive for the candidates. Less than 55% of the eligible citizens vote. There are lobbying systems where most of the legislation is influenced by huge amounts of money swaying the legislators to vote a certain way. A gerrymandered system ensures that voting districts are reshaped to increase the chance that any incumbent legislator will be elected again and again.

WHAT CAN WE DO TO IMPROVE THE OPERATION OF OUR DEMOCRACY?

In 2015, the League of Women Voters (LWV) cited three problems that are weakening democracy:

- Congressional districts are drawn and gerrymandered to benefit self-serving politicians.
- Access to voting is being limited and denied.
- 'Dark money' is infiltrating elections so voters don't even know who is bankrolling the political messages that we see and hear.

The League said: 'We should not stand by as our democracy falls into the iron-fisted grip of billionaires, special interests, and the political machines they fund.' The League, along with other groups, raise money to correct these problems and make democracy work better.[8]

HOW DO CITIZENS VIEW GOVERNMENT?

We have to also ask how citizens view their government. Americans are prone to boast about American exceptionalism and American democracy. This has led America to believe that the rest of the world admires its system and that America holds a duty to bring democracy and freedom to every country. Iraq and Afghanistan are said to be invaded to bring about freedom in those countries, and America preaches its system to Africa and Asia, totally ignoring the differences in their cultures and beliefs.

These faults are becoming visible to Americans and the rest of the world. Citizens may experience incompetent government workers and bureaucracies; a judiciary that delays or fails to dispense justice; a system of continuous clashes or gridlock between the President and the Congress or between the two major parties; a police force that is abusive; local politicians who use the political system to feather their own nest; or a government that doesn't address the main problems such as immigration or expensive medical care or a deteriorating infrastructure but instead kicks these problems down the road. Americans cannot be pleased with their public school students' low ratings in science and math compared to students in other leading countries; or that their health system costs significantly more than other countries' health systems without any better results. The U.S. ranks 49th in life expectancy and 173 in infant mortality. No wonder the Pew Research Center pointed out that our citizens' belief in American exceptionalism had declined ten points since 2011.[9]

The trouble with believing in American exceptionalism is that it neglects infrastructure and taxes, and meanwhile much is spent on projecting power abroad in an ever expanding defense budget. The priorities appear wrong, and from time to time voices arise to plead that foreign involvement be reduced in favor of focusing on the nation's economy and American society. The argument is that if American society was improved, this would contribute more to the view of genuine American leadership and exceptionalism than just spending so much money on broadcasting an image of U.S. power overseas.

America has to recognize that world leadership is today being shared with a number of countries, including China, India, Russia, and others. It has a poor history of collaborating with other countries on international agreements such as regulating pollution (by not signing the Kyoto Treaty), refusing to strengthen the ban on biological weapons, and not joining the ban on land mines or the use of napalm and cluster bombs. If America is going to be part of the international community, it can't continue to exempt itself from following the moral and legal standards held in common by many other nations.[10] It needs to work more collaboratively with other strong nations rather than alone.

Consider the poster put out by the Occupy Wall Street group that provocatively raised the following points:

•   In the Nordic countries—Sweden, Norway, Denmark, Finland—education is tuition-free including at universities. Nordic governments go further and give a monthly allowance to help university students cover their living expenses. Although this results in higher taxes, Nordic students are better educated. Their free education reduces social inequality and benefits both individuals and society in the long run.

- In the U.S., college students incur crippling debt to become educated and they enter their work life burdened by this debt.
- The U.S. has more people in prison than in any other country and spends more money on its prisons than on its college students.
- The rich own most of the politicians, who are able to fool young men into fighting in military engagements.[11]

The Occupy Wall Street group forgot to mention how many guns are found in the U.S., how much sugar, salt, and fat is found in most of our food products, and how litigious and costly our judicial system is.

So how exceptional is America? A 2016 report prepared by U.S. News & World Report, WPP's BAV Consulting and the Wharton School of the University of Pennsylvania named the 'Best Countries' in the world, based on ratings in 24 categories. Germany was first, Canada second, the United Kingdom third, with the U.S. ranking fourth, followed by Sweden fifth.[12] Another study, by scholars from the Harvard Business School and Duke University, asked Americans which country they would prefer to live in. They were shown the income distribution of country A and B (and were not told the countries, which were actually Sweden and the U.S.). About 90% of Americans preferred to live in country A—the one with the Swedish income distribution![13]

It is true that the American brand and mix of democracy and capitalism deliver many great outcomes—the U.S. is the richest and most powerful country in the world with a high standard of living. But there are many questionable features that we will examine in the next ten chapters.

NOTES

1 See: www.answers.com/Q/How_many_countries_have_democratic_form_of_gov ernment. (accessed 03.03.16).
2 See: Wikipedia, 'Democracy Index,' March 16, 2015.
3 See: https://freedomhouse.org/report/freedom-world/freedom-world-2014#.VQb wtI7F-PZ, (accessed 03.03.16).
4 Bello, 'Cleaning up Latin American Democracy', *The Economist*, March 28, 2015.
5 L. Lessig, *Republic, Lost: How Money Corrupts Congress – and a Plan to Stop It* (Hachette, New York, 2011).
6 See: www.publicintegrity.org/2012/10/18/11527/citizens-united-decision-and-why-it-matters (accessed 03.03.16).

7 See: www.semipresidentialism.com/?p=195 (accessed 03.03.16).

8 Mailed letter from Elisabeth MacNamara, President of the League of Women Voters in 2015.

9 C. M. Blow, 'Who Loves America?', *New York Times*, February 23, 2015.

10 See: J. R. Orenstein, *Fixing American Government* (Sun Coast Digital Press, Satasota, FL, 2015).

11 Occupy Posters: owsposters.tumblr.com.

12 A. Boult, 'UK Named the Third Best Country in the World', *Daily Telegraph*, January 20, 2016.

13 N. D. Kristof, 'Why Let the Rich Hoard All the Toys', *New York Times*, October 3, 2012.

CHAPTER 2

REFORMING ELECTIONS—WHY ARE CITIZENS NOT VOTING?

'They who have no voice nor vote in the electing of representatives, do not enjoy liberty, but are absolutely enslaved to those who have votes.'
Benjamin Franklin, 1774

'Let the people rule.'
Andrew Jackson

'Democracy is not a spectator sport, it's a participatory event. If we don't participate in it, it ceases to be democracy.'
Michael Moore

emocracies have their starting point with elections. If there are no elections, the political system is not democratic. Such a political system is run by a monarch or an authoritarian figure or group or by a one-party system.

Even if a country runs candidates and elections, the political system may still not be democratic. This would be the case if only one candidate or selected candidates run and/or if there are limits on who could vote or the effort to vote is made costly to specific voters because of difficult registration or threats.

Let's start with the question of *voters* and who can vote. Then we will turn to the question of *candidates* and who can run and how they can get elected in a democracy.

WHAT IS A CITIZEN?

Before defining a voter, we must first define a citizen. A citizen is a person who legally belongs to a country and has the rights and privileges and protection of that country. Usually the person is a native or naturalized member of that country and owes allegiance to that country. That person also has responsibilities as a citizen, such as accepting and following the laws and requirements of that country.

WHICH CITIZENS CAN VOTE?

Not all citizens in a nation may be allowed to vote. In ancient Athens, only 1 in 5 citizens could vote. Youth, women, and slaves could not vote. In the U.S., many framers of the Constitution did not think that most people should vote. They worried about voter ignorance and demagogic politicians. They preferred that voting rights went to property owners and white males. Slaves could not vote until they were freed by the Emancipation Proclamation in January 1, 1863. Even then, ex-slaves had to pay a poll tax in the Deep South and many worried about being lynched.

American women did not have the right to vote until the passage of the 19th Amendment on May 19, 1919. Agitation for women's rights started in the 1840s along with the push to free slaves. Women had few rights at home. Her husband was the master. He took all the rights to her property. She could not go to college. She could not enter most professions. She could not get a divorce. These and other inequities were headlined in the Declaration of Sentiments passed at the Women's Rights Convention on July 19–20, 1848. Yet 70 more years passed before women were granted the right to vote.

Each country must define who can vote. They must define the age at which a person can start voting as an adult. In a full democracy, there would be no voting limitations based on the person's race, income, property, gender, or other criteria. A big issue today is whether citizens who are ex-offenders should be allowed to vote. The rules differ from state to state. Because most ex-offenders might have grown up poor and are more likely to vote Democratic, Republicans are more likely to oppose voting by ex-offenders.

The U.S. Constitution actually doesn't contain a statement that every citizen has a right to vote. It only states that voting rights cannot be abrogated on the basis of race or gender discrimination. But a State may insist that a citizen bring along an ID when he or she comes to vote. Two Representatives in Congress are proposing a constitutional amendment stating that, 'every citizen of the United States, who is of legal voting age, shall have the fundamental right to vote in any public election held in the jurisdiction in which the citizen resides.'

HOW MANY CITIZENS VOTE?

Given the right and privilege to vote, it is surprising how many citizens choose not to vote. Considering that all citizens will be affected by new laws, rules, and regulations, one would expect all citizens to want to elect representatives who will carry out their interests. Voters periodically need to decide which representatives deserve to be continued and which should be replaced. Voting in community, city, and state elections should be important to citizens. And voting in federal elections every two years should be very important to citizens.

Yet in the U.S., voter turnout is disappointingly low. U.S. presidential elections are held every four years and voting age since 1972 has been set at 18 and above. The percentage of eligible voters who voted was 51.21% in 2000; 56.70% in 2004; 58.23% in 2008; and 54.87% in 2012. Rarely does the percentage rise above 60%.[1] Yet in other free countries, citizens vote in much larger numbers: Austria, 75%; Belgium, 89%; and Germany, 71%. In the mid-term two year elections, an even smaller percentage of citizens cast a vote (just 36.4%). Clearly, the mid-term elections draw less voter interest dealing as they do with the election of House and Senate nominees.

There are other differences in the voting percentage. By U.S. states, Maine had the highest turnout with 59% in 2012, and Indiana had the lowest voting percentage at just 28%. There is variation by income level, with the more highly educated and higher income groups turning out to vote at a higher percentage. In recent elections, voter turnout rates for women have equaled or exceeded voter turnout rates for men.

By race, there are variations. In 2012, the black percentage vote exceeded for the first time the white percentage vote (Pew Research Center 2013, Jeff Oren). By contrast, Hispanics vote at a disappointing rate. Their families don't talk much about politics. They often feel the candidates don't really care about Hispanics or their issues. Yet as more Hispanics get older, it is expected that more will vote.[2]

The future hinges on how Millennials (those aged 18–34) will vote. One recent poll showed just over one-quarter described themselves as strong Democrats or Republicans, and 40% described themselves as independent. Many seemed to be losing faith in electoral politics as a way to tackle society's problems. Of course, this can change when exciting candidates appear, such as Bill Clinton, Barack Obama, or Bernie Sanders.[3]

The percentage of voter-age citizens who decide to vote is also influenced by other factors, such as the interest generated by the two presidential candidates, the importance of some issues to the voters, and the amount spent in election contests, which is growing every cycle.

In some countries, notably Australia, voting is mandatory. Australia fines a non-voter about $15. Naomi Wolf, the social critic, wants voting to be mandatory in the U.S. too. Citizens would not be able to renew their auto registration or file taxes unless they showed that they had voted in elections.[4] Mandatory voting would transform our country. The people who tend not to vote are young, lower income, more immigrant and minor groups. Their votes would largely go to the Democrats. This helps explain why the Republicans are so active in trying to require voters' IDs and taking other steps to make voting by certain groups more difficult.

WHY DO SO MANY CITIZENS NOT VOTE?

Is the low voting level a sign that people are content, or that they are highly discontent and believe that voting won't make a difference to their life or the lives of others they care about? But as Pericles said of non-voters back in 430 B.C., 'Just because you do not take an interest in politics doesn't mean politics won't take an interest in you.'

Citizens have many reasons not to vote:

- My vote won't make any difference. It would be one vote out of millions.
- The country is run and ruled by powerful rich people and my vote won't make a difference;.
- There are so many names on the ballot that I can't possibly know much about them and make an informed choice.
- The two political parties are similar and it doesn't matter who wins. Neither is addressing the real issues. Or the two parties are so different that they can't agree on anything and nothing gets done.
- Choosing to vote costs me money and time. I have to leave work, travel, stand in line for a long time, all for a vote that doesn't count much.

Cynicism also plays a role in many citizens not voting. Many Americans live lives of low pay and little hope. They don't believe that politicians will help improve their lives. The fact is that mobility has declined in American society. Americans rightfully boasted in the past that America is the 'land of opportunity.' But America has become a more rigid society. Although Senator Marco Rubio would say 'We are a nation of haves and soon-to-haves,' it is more true that America is becoming a nation of 'haves and have-nots.' The U.S. today has less economic mobility than Canada and much of Europe. A child born in the bottom fifth of incomes has only a 4% chance of rising to the top fifth. There is a high correlation between the family's income and their children's chance for achieving a good income.[5]

Those who end up voting are not a real cross-section of the population. Those who vote tend to be more middle class, or more ideological, or most single-issue driven, or more active in their party. The poor and many other groups are underrepresented.

We live in a period of great cynicism about politicians and government. The politicians appear to be in it for the money and the power. They are all funded by special interests and the public good is furthest from their minds. Seventeen candidates entered the race to be the next Republican President. Among these candidates, one stood out greatly from the other candidates as an "outsider." That was Donald Trump, a vain, egotistical, and self-centered man, who commanded the most news coverage and who was the most outspoken. He defied "political correctness" by proposing that all illegal Mexicans be sent home and that we build a wall to be paid for by Mexico to keep further illegal Mexicans out; that we ban Muslims from entering our country; along with other discriminations that run counter to American beliefs and ideals. Yet every new issue in his "politics of disgust" seems to get him more votes. He attracts many low income and angry groups who feel downtrodden, neglected by established politicians and parties and who want a fresh voice to represent their grievances. Trump is a rare and original phenomenon in American politics who has unnerved large swathes of the established conservative Republican party. He is hardly a person to entrust with the future of not only 350,000,000 Americans but largely the fate of the entire human race.

IS THERE ACTIVE VOTER SUPPRESSION?

Over 50 years ago, President Lyndon Johnson signed the Voting Rights Act of 1965 to prohibit racial discrimination in voting. Before this act, voting rights were guaranteed by the 14th and 15th Amendments but racial discrimination had persisted. Section 2 of the 1965 Voting Rights Act prohibits state and local government from imposing any voting law that discriminates against racial or language minorities. The Act specifically outlaws literacy tests and other devices that historically disenfranchised racial minorities. The 1965 Voting Rights Act was a major piece of civil rights legislation to correct this situation and it led to a mass enfranchisement of black voters. It also led the Democrats to lose the South.

Congress had repeatedly reaffirmed the act with additional protections. In 2006, Congress overwhelmingly extended the Act for another 25 years. But in 2013, the Supreme Court concluded in a 5–4 decision in *Shelby County v. Holder* that federal oversight of states and localities with a history of racial discrimination was no longer needed. They concluded that the Voting Rights Act had done its job and was not longer required.

True, literacy tests and poll taxes had been eliminated. But a determined group of conservatives in many states started to introduce other measures to keep black citizens, who typically vote Democratic, from voting. State and local areas in North Carolina, Texas, and five other states tightened up laws against voting. They introduced requirements for voter identification (a birth certificate, proof of address, and possibly an auto license) and they cut back early voting and same-day registration. Their legislators claimed that these measures were necessary because of extensive voter fraud and to increase efficiency in polling. Yet there was no evidence of voter fraud.

This voting suppression activity continued into 2015 with Wisconsin Governor Scott Walker reducing early voting and making it more difficult for college students to vote; ex-Governor Jeb Bush trying to purge Florida voter rolls; and New Jersey Governor Chris Christie vetoed a bill to expand early voting in New Jersey. In the last case, New Jersey had one of the lowest voter turnouts in elections, something like 20–30%. Christie opposes automatic voter registration because he worries that it would lead to more vote fraud. There is more to it: 'I think they're afraid of more Obamas getting elected to office,' says the Rev. Dr. Earl Johnson of Raleigh, North Carolina.

Ironically, in Texas, 90-year-old former House Speaker Jim Wright was denied a voter ID card at a Texas Department of Public Safety Office. He had to make a special trip to get a State of Texas Election Identification Certificate when he realized that Texas would not accept his Texas driver's license that expired in 2010 and his Texas Christian University faculty ID. If it is hard for a former Speaker of the House to get the right to vote, one can imagine how many other people will have difficulty.

Between 2011 and 2015, *395 new voting restrictions were proposed in 49 states.* Career politicians design these restrictions to manipulate district lines and deny millions of Americans the right to vote. Voting rights are necessary to build a government that works for the people.

By 2015, State actions to limit voting by citizens had already come to the attention of the Supreme Court. The Court rejected an appeal from Arizona and Kansas to require evidence of citizenship. The Court refused to let states require evidence of citizenship when people register to vote for federal elections. The plaintiffs, including the North Carolina NAACP, the League of Women Voters, and a host of African-American churches, sought to prove that the law's intent is to disenfranchise minority voters, not reduce alleged voter fraud.[6]

HOW WELL INFORMED ARE VOTERS?

All that we can hope for is that citizens vote and that they are well informed to choose candidates who would represent their interests and desires. Many voters are not well informed; they are poorly educated and do not read or keep up with current events and issues. Mark Twain gave his impression of the usefulness of newspapers: 'If you don't read the newspaper you are uninformed; if you do read the newspaper you are misinformed.'

Naomi Wolf recently reported that one-third of the American population could not name one branch of government; two-thirds couldn't name two branches of government. Many voters never had a course in civics or remember any of it. She recommended that an annual National Issues Day is held at a large gathering called a Citizens Assembly.[7] Consider the following: According to *The New American Democracy*, 'barely a third of the citizenry can recall the name of their [U.S. House of Representatives] representative, and even fewer can remember anything he or she has done for the district. Only about one in ten people can remember how their representative voted on a particular bill.' According to the *American Thinker*, only 27% of citizens can name both of their U.S. Senators.[8]

Even citizens who have benefitted from a good education find it hard to know what the main issues are and to have an opinion on how their representatives will or should vote. The U.S. proliferates in media and opinion leaders who differ greatly in their political positions. The *New York Times* represents a liberal Democratic position while the *Wall Street Journal* represents a conservative Republican position. Radio stations abound with commentators on the left and even more on the right. Every citizen ends up with reading or listening to some favored media and ignores media representing the other side. Everyone lives in a bubble.

The result is that most voters end up identifying with a political party and feel that this party well defines that voter's preferences and interests. One of the main reasons for political parties is to enable voters to avoid the work of researching issues. They can leave it to their chosen party to define their interests. We might argue that citizens are not thinking machines: They are feeling machines that think occasionally.[9]

Yet there remain about 20% of U.S. citizens who claim to be independent voters who may sometimes vote Democratic and sometimes Republican. As such, they are an important voting group in a democracy because they can impact on who gets elected. I would go further and say that the larger the group of independent voters, the more democratic is the political system.

DO VOTERS VOTE ON THEIR BEST INTERESTS?

Poorer voters who benefit from social assistance programs do not always vote for the Democratic Party. Recently some blue states (Democratic) have been turning red (Republican). The state of Maine, which is among the poorest U.S. states, re-elected its strongly anti-welfare Republican governor. Kentucky, another poor state, elected a Republican governor who vowed to undo the Medicaid expansion in spite of this state having the largest increase in coverage under Obamacare.[10]

How do we understand why some people vote against their own interests? The first observation is that many poor people don't even show up to vote. They may have paid little or no attention to political news and may find it hard to register or costly to take time off. Some poor people who do vote may feel that the Democratic Party is anti-religious or pro-abortion and that they should vote as a protest. Or they may have witnessed others who are getting social assistance abuse it, like seeing a food-stamp person they know eat in an expensive steak restaurant or a person with disability spending his time fishing. Many people receiving some social assistance may look down on others who are getting too much and want to dissociate themselves from that class. Some may think that the Republican Party will create or save more real jobs and produce more economic growth than the Democrats. It is a major challenge for Democratic Party workers to canvass their often rural districts and convince these citizens to vote and view the Democratic Party as doing more to meet their interests than the Republican Party.

DOES THE MAJORITY VOTE ALWAYS WIN?

The other question has to do with the meaning of a majority vote. We normally mean that a proposal wins if it gets more than 50% of the eligible votes. Yet there are occasions when a two-thirds vote is required to pass a bill. This is a higher standard and reduces the chance for passage. Things are more likely to stay the same in a voting area that requires a two-thirds vote for passage. The two-thirds level appeals more to conservative voters who don't like to see much change. *But this means that one-third or more of our Congress can prevent a vote that a majority of the country is strongly in favor of.*

If a majority rule of over 50% operates, what insures that minority groups in the population will have their rights respected? Democracies must make sure that minorities have the same rights as majorities and receive fair treatment. As an example, suppose a community with mostly Christians vote against allowing a mosque to be built in its area. They cannot pressure the small number of

Muslims in the area to become Christians. But Muslims have the right to run meetings inviting Christians to listen to their case. Over time, Muslims might get the needed support from enough Christians to permit a mosque to be built in their area.

HOW TO MAKE THE VOTING PROCESS MORE EFFICIENT

Most voting takes place today in local polling centers. Paper balloting continues to be the most frequently used media. After the polls are closed, a lot of careful vote counting takes place. This has led to another proposal, namely using electronic balloting machines made by a variety of manufacturers. This would count the votes much faster. Yet in spite of the apparent advantages, e-machines have found limited use. People have to be shown how to vote electronically. The polling place will have fewer electronic machines than if it used its space for paper balloting. Most importantly, questions have been raised about the reliability of these machines and whether they are tamper-proof. In early 2014, the Presidential Commission on Election Administration issued a report forewarning an impending crisis from outmoded voting machines. Listed were these problems:

- 36 states purchased a majority of machines before 2006; 43 states use systems that are no longer manufactured.
- 28 states' systems were not certified by the federal Election Assistance Commission because they predate standards.
- Aging machines often are prone to crashes and screen freezes, sometimes sending voters home and losing their vote.

The social critic Naomi Wolf would ban all electronic voting. She wants everything to be hand counted. She would ban all private vendors from playing any role in the voting process. She would ban all state requirements for state-issued IDs at the polls. She would put all polling places under video surveillance to spot voter fraud and monitor election personnel and track the turnout. She would make election fraud a major felony with prison time and huge fines for repeat offenders. She would want persons on their 18th birthday to register at any post office. Finally, she would have Election Day declared a federal holiday, requiring all employers to allow their workers time to vote. Clearly, she is issuing a call for cities and states to carefully rethink their voting system and change it to make it easier for more citizens to vote almost at a zero cost to them.[11] We must realize that citizens who have had bad experiences or long waits or high costs may give up on the idea of voting next time.

The great need is to make it easier for citizens to vote. Why does everyone have to vote on the same Tuesday every two years? Historically, Tuesday was chosen when the U.S. was largely an agricultural society: Tuesday occurred between the end of the Sunday Sabbath and before the Thursday markets opened. It has been suggested that if the presidential election has to be on a Tuesday every four years, that Tuesday should be declared a national holiday so that more workers could vote without losing pay. A much better time would be the weekend when many workers aren't at work. It has been suggested that voting could take place between 2 p.m. on Saturday and 6 p.m. on Sunday, thereby not affecting any Sabbath. Or the voting could take place at Walmart or Costco or in huge stadiums where there is adequate parking space. To encourage more voting, a lottery ticket could be distributed to every voter but the winner had to show that he or she had voted.

Now that we live in a digital world where information can be sent and received instantly, why do we still use a voting process requiring citizens to take time off from work and travel to a polling center, to wait in long lines to be registered and to be given a form to take into a private voting booth to tick off their favorite candidates, return the form, and then leave the polling center. Why not let citizens vote whenever and wherever they want? They could ask for an early ballot and mail it in. Today 27 states and Washington, D.C. allow voters to vote by mail if they prefer. Every requesting voter is sent their ballot in the mail several weeks before the election to fill in and send back. Or the ballot may come to their email address and they send it in. Why, in a digital world, should voting be limited to a certain time and place?

Even voter registration could be improved. When students reach 17 years of age, they would be notified to pre-register so that they could vote when they reach 18 years of age. Another suggestion is that when young persons apply for a driver's license, they should automatically receive voter registration at the same time. All of this would definitely lead to more voters voting every two years.

In summary, there is a need to expand early voting, absentee voting, and same-day registration.

WHO ARE THE POLITICAL CANDIDATES AND HOW DO THEY GET ELECTED?

In any democratic society, certain people decide that they want a political career. They want to run for a political office such as a mayor, governor, Representative, or Senator. They may feel that they have good ideas for making government work better for more people. Or they may see this as an opportunity to gain some power, fame, or fortune.

Rarely will a political candidate run as an independent with no party affiliation. Joining a political party provides the candidate with an identity, a set of believers and followers, and a source of funds. Even joining a political party does not mean the party will support his or her candidacy because the person may be one of many seeking a particular office. If the person is the only one seeking that office, he or she will be the candidate. Otherwise, the person will have to compete for that office by doing a better job of impressing the members of the party and the voters. More than 16 people in the Republican Party threw their hats in to run for President in November 2016.

The U.S. has a two-party system, the Democrats and the Republicans. The Democrats represent more the working class and the Republicans represent more the business interests and the rich. This split between the Left and the Right is found in many countries. But many countries have more than two parties operating. France, for example, has the Socialist Party, the Greens, the Left Party, the Radical Party of the Left, the Union for a Popular Movement, the New Centre, and the National Front. This means that a candidate normally has to belong to one party and form a coalition agreement with other parties. Often two stable coalitions emerge, one on the center-left and the other on the center-right.

The U.S. has had third parties from time to time, such as the Socialist Party under Norman Thomas, the Bull-Moose Party under Teddy Roosevelt, the Greenback Party, and the Prohibition Party. In 2012, Robert David Steele ran for President of the Reform Party to overcome 'the tyranny of the two party system.' But despite his efforts in attracting smaller parties to join him in a People Reform Coalition, each small party wanted to massage its own ego. Understandably, most third parties tend to disappear. They arise again when the policies of the two main parties are too similar and a political candidate emerges to form an independent party.[12] Virtually all politically motivated persons will affiliate with one of the two major parties and work hard to get recognized and to rise in the ranks. Most will be lawyers and some will be successful business people, and occasionally a physician or an academic might run for office.

The candidate will move through a number of steps on the way to becoming electable. First, the candidate will have to test the waters by getting the support of families, friends, and the chosen political party. A big challenge is to raise enough money to support printing brochures, running ads, swinging through the areas, and getting known and favored. The other challenge is to develop a powerful message to win the votes of the party against the party's other candidate seeking the same office. The candidate needs to gather enough signatures to run in the party primary. If the candidate manages to win in the party primary, the candidate must run against the candidate from the other party for that position. This calls for renewed fundraising and revising the message and campaign for a larger voting public. If the candidate wins against the other candidate, the candidate is now the holder of the office, and must prove that he or she can do a good job in that office.

THE PARTY TRIES TO CHOOSE THE BEST CANDIDATE AMONG SEVERAL

A political party can suffer from one of two situations: Either it cannot find a satisfactory candidate willing to run, or it has too many candidates to choose from. In the former case, the party will try to draft some capable person. Some of the most capable candidates don't want to run for office. Many are CEOs of huge multinational companies earning $10 million a year. Why would they want to earn only $400,000 a year as the U.S. President and suffer from excessive probing by journalists and abuse by members of the opposing party? If they agree to run, they would want to set the terms on which they will run. This means that the party's candidate may depart from the party's position on a number of issues.

Imagine if the Republican Party wanted ex-NYC city mayor Michael Bloomberg to be their candidate. He is very popular with the public. But Bloomberg is against the Republican positions on guns and immigration. He would lose at the primary because of the more extreme Republicans. The party has to decide whether it prefers an inferior loyal party candidate or a strong more independent candidate to put before the public. The political parties had more power in the old days when they chose the candidate in a smoke-filled room away from the public's eye.

The party also has a problem when there are too many candidates seeking to win the primary. Let's examine the 2016 situation where 17 Republican candidates announced that they would run for President. This has not happened before. It is a sign that the Republican Party has no clear winner or leader. Were it to have such a leader, there would be far fewer candidates. The large number poses some problems:

- First, the candidates will obviously disagree on a number of issues with each other, leading the public to wonder if the party has any strong or clear position on a number of important issues. Eventually, the candidates start bad-mouthing each other hoping to gain some 'voter share.'
- Second, the party has no control over who chooses to run. In 2016, many Republicans were embarrassed about candidate Donald Trump. They were embarrassed about his attacks on Mexicans, Muslims, and women. They were more embarrassed to see his position improve with each carefully crafted insult. One Republican called Trump a 'wrecking ball.' But the Republican Party could not tell Donald Trump not to run: If they did, he might start a third party and even hurt their chances more in 2016.
- Third, the party has to choose a fair way to let each candidate describe his or her views. In 2016, the Republican Party chose the top ten candidate vote-getters for the big show and the six poorer vote-getters for a smaller show. Three moderators from Fox each put different questions to specific candidates.[13] More Republican presidential debates occurred to further winnow out some candidates.

It is truly difficult for voters to know who would make the best presidential candidate. If one were to look at Churchill or Lincoln as young men, would it seem likely that they would both become charismatic, effective leaders? What makes a great leader? Did they become great leaders because they lived in trying times? We should at least look for certain qualities such as wisdom, integrity, a sense of honor, altruism, and simple tenacity. We need signs of good character but also of street smarts.

HOW DO THE FINAL POLITICAL CANDIDATES GET SELECTED?

In each presidential election, the presidential candidates tour several of the states to meet voters and speak about their policies and promises. By tradition, the first two states that presidential candidates canvas are Iowa and New Hampshire. These states were selected by the political parties and it would take a very determined group to try to change this sequence of states. Iowa is not a very representative state in that 98% of the voters are white and the large majority are rural. The state of Georgia would be a much better representative state to start off the political canvassing. New Hampshire meanwhile is a very small state whose best virtue is that the candidates can easily cover this state.

Each candidate will set up offices in each part of the state and speak in as many locations as possible. The candidate's staff will choose a venue and build an audience where the candidate can speak. In 2016, presidential candidate

Ted Cruz says he visited every part of Iowa. On a stated date, a caucus or a primary will take place. Iowa does the voting by caucus. Registered members of that political party (in a closed caucus) will gather in the evening in each precinct, chat with each other, move into separate groups to indicate which candidate they prefer. New Hampshire does it by running a primary election. All registered members of the party vote on ballots to choose their preferred candidate. A count will be taken of the votes for each candidate and each precinct will send its vote breakdown to the party's headquarters in that state. By the next morning, it will be known which candidate in each party won that state.

Caucuses and primaries are repeated in the remaining states, and this determines the number of delegates for each candidate sent to the political party's national convention which takes place in the summer. At the Democratic convention, the number of state delegates is proportional to the number of votes received in the state primary or caucus. The Republican Party, however, allows states to use either a winner-takes-all system or a proportional system. Ultimately, votes are taken of the delegates at the party's national convention to determine which candidate the party will nominate as its presidential candidate.

Following the selection of the presidential candidate for each political party, there will be a number of nationally televised debates between the two candidates for the public to see and hear in making up their minds. On November 8 of that presidential year, the voters will determine the next President of the U.S.

THE CHANGING ROLE OF THE MEDIA IN INFORMING AND INFLUENCING VOTERS

Before the digital revolution, most citizens got their news from our three main broadcast networks of ABC, CBS, and NBC. Each network's revenue came from its advertisers, who didn't want the networks to show partisanship to either party. The advertisers didn't care whether they were selling their wares to Democrats or Republicans. So the networks essentially saw their job to be to supply fairly objective news to all the nation's citizens, not to special interest groups.

As for local newspapers, all of them served up the same news, although there might have been some slanting in how each news items was reported. The *New York Times* carried a more liberal slant while the *Wall Street Journal* and the *Chicago Tribune* carried a more conservative slant. Popular magazines such as

Time and *Newsweek* carried largely unbiased news presentations. If some readers wanted to consume more liberal or conservative news, they could always find some magazines that were distinctively liberal or conservative.

Today's voters have a choice of thousands of different online and offline sources of information and opinion. Voters preferring conservative news opinion will watch Fox and liberals will watch MSNBC. Both are biased sources of information and opinion. Today the conservative Fox has a far larger audience than the more unbiased ABC, CBS, and NBC put together. Voters are increasingly choosing to read and listen to the media that fits their political leanings. Voters grow more tribal over time, unable to know or appreciate the opinions of other tribes. The nation becomes more and more divided, not only at the national level but also at the state, city, and neighborhood level.

Many stories come out that are actually untrue but deeply believed in by the partisans. One story claimed that family planning agencies sell the flesh of aborted unborn babies. Even when a fact-checking agency proves this as patently false, most people don't hear this or continue to believe this. Instead of having a well-educated citizenry sharing a common heritage, the U.S. consists of multiple tribes who live and breathe different versions of the truth.

THE INCREASING ROLE OF MONEY IN VOTING CAMPAIGNS

The amount of money being spent in today's U.S. elections is obscene. The Koch brothers announced that they plan to spend close to $900 million influencing the 2016 political campaign. Just imagine if the two Koch brothers suddenly had an epiphany and instead decided to fund education reform and lower the cost of student loans with that money. If the billions being spent on elections could be diverted to any of many needy social causes, the whole country would be better off and the donors could be justifiably proud of their beneficence, as were Andrew Carnegie, the Rockefellers, and the Fords proud of their contributions to improving American lives in the past.

Hillary Clinton, in her presidential run, said, 'I will do everything I can to appoint Supreme Court justices who protect the right to vote and *do not protect the right of billionaires to buy elections*.' The activist group Move to Amend, intent on overturning the nefarious Supreme Court's *Citizens United* decision, made the following observation:

> Corporations are not merely exercising political power today—they have become de facto ruling institutions. Ultra-wealthy individuals and unelected,

unaccountable corporate CEOs make the fundamental public policy decisions in this country. They decide the levels of toxins and poisons that will be in our air and water, what work we do and how much we get paid to do it, what kind of health care we get, and what our country's energy policy will be. 'We the People' get to decide between Coke or Pepsi and paper or plastic at the grocery store. Citizens are treated as consumers or workers but rarely as sovereign human beings with the right to decide how our society will be organized.[14]

In 2014, nearly $5 billion was spent by candidates, political parties, PACs, and nonprofit groups to influence elections. About 20% of donations came from hidden donors through Super PACs and special interest organizations receiving money from corporations, unions, and wealthy individuals from the US and abroad. The estimate is that nearly $10 billion will be spent on elections in 2016.

A Brief History of U.S. Campaign Finance

We need to take a brief look at the history of U.S. campaign finance to understand how we got to today's grotesque situation. Professor Roger Berkowitz summarized the U.S. history of campaign finance and campaign finance reform in seven stages (with an eighth added):

1   During the 1787 Constitutional Convention, the big issue was corruption. The founding fathers didn't want legislators to hold civil office while serving as a legislator or using their post to enrich themselves or their friends. They also chose to limit members of the House of Representatives to two years so that they would not form strong alliances with members of the Executive branch.

2   The second stage runs from the passage of the Constitution until the election of Andrew Jackson in 1828. Candidates largely paid for their own campaign expenses, which covered printing campaign pamphlets and paying for some food and drink at rallies. The candidates were generally well-off and aimed to get votes from propertied white men.

3   The third stage began in 1828 with the election of Andrew Jackson. Jackson was the first to aim his appeal directly to voters and not simply to party elites. This required a lot more money and Jackson raised the funds from those who were seeking jobs in the government. This was the beginning of the spoils system where current and prospective government employees essentially financed the election.

4   The fourth stage included the spoils system until the passage of the Pendleton Act in 1883 which established the Federal Civil Service,

requiring civil service applicants to take and pass exams to get a government job. It outlawed the spoils system and politicians needed new sources of funds. They solicited wealthy individuals and corporations. The era of corporate funding came into being and corporations took great advantage of their influence over Congress and the voters.

5   The fifth stage consisted of Teddy Roosevelt pushing Congress to pass the Tillman Act in 1907, which terminated as illegal all corporate campaign contributions. The Tillman Act carried penalties for its violation but it did not institute enforcement rules. Many violations and scandals occurred.

6   The sixth stage consisted of the passage of the Federal Election Campaign Act (FECA) in 1974. FECA limited individual contributions to individual candidates to $1,000 and PACs were limited to $5,000 to an individual candidate; limited how much candidates could spend on a campaign; established the public financing of campaigns that required a voluntary limit on campaign expenditures; required that candidates, parties, PACs, and groups engaging in express advocacy disclose their fundraising and spending; and created the Federal Election Commission to regulate and enforce the new rules. In 1976, the Supreme Court in *Buckley v. Valeo* struck down compulsory limits on spending both by individual candidates and by PACs and other groups. The Court wanted to recognize the right of free speech by individuals and corporations while acknowledging that large contributions is a kind of *quid pro quo* corruption. The Court ruled that general expenditures not coordinated with a specific candidate were legal. The result was that money given to political parties and other groups was not subject to the limits imposed on individual contributions to individual candidates. PACs used large sums of 'soft money' that bordered on influence peddling, although the money was not given to individual candidates. By 2001–2002, the Democratic Party took in $200 million and the Republicans $421 million.

7   The seventh stage consisted of Congress trying again to restrain the avalanche of money in 2002 by passing the Bi-Partisan Campaign Reform Act (BCRA) (also known as the McCain-Feingold Act). BRCA prohibited unlimited soft money contributions by corporations and unions. But in 2010, the Supreme Court ruled in *Citizens United* that 'corporations are people' and removed the prohibition and allowed unlimited soft money to flow. Justice Anthony Kennedy' argued that associations such as corporations and unions are guaranteed by the 1st Amendment the right to engage in political speech and the law should not muffle the voices of significant segments of the economy. He was echoing Felix Frankfurter's argument that, 'the expression of bloc sentiment has always been an integral part of our democratic and legislative processes.' Yet a *Washington Post*-ABC News poll shortly thereafter found that roughly 80% of

(Continued)

(Continued)

Americans opposed the *Citizens United* ruling. A grassroots bipartisan group called Move to Amend formed to gather support for a constitutional amendment overturning the two main concepts: (1) Corporations are not persons with inalienable rights, and (2) the spending of money to influence elections is not speech under the 1st Amendment.[15]

8   In April, 2014, the Supreme Court issued a 5–4 ruling that restricting how much money a donor may spend in total to all candidates or committees violated the 1st Amendment. So instead of arriving at a sound campaign finance law, the Supreme Court by a narrow 5–4 decision declared that limits on campaign expenditures are unconstitutional. Many groups have pressed Mary Jo White, Chair of the Securities and Exchange Commission (SEC), to require corporations to inform their shareholders how much political money is being spent, but she has consistently resisted doing this. 'Dark money' continues to move into PACs and Super PACs without citizens knowing who the donors are.

Today an aspiring presidential candidate will need a lot of money to finance the candidate's primary election campaign and more money if the candidate becomes the party's nominee for the highest office. According to Elizabeth Drew, a presidential candidate would need three things to make a serious run: (1) One billionaire who likes and will finance the candidate; (2) a Super PAC that claims to be an independent PAC ready to accept large 'hard money' donations that have to be disclosed; and (3) a nonprofit organization that operates exclusively to promote social welfare. This last group can collect 'soft' money (called 'dark money') because the donors' names don't have to be disclosed.[16] It is even possible that foreign money flows into PACs and Super PACs without the donor names becoming public.

The money coming into the Super PACs is used by the political committees to hire lawyers, researchers, and speechwriters, and to pay for chartered planes, luxury hotel suites, and sundry expenses. Any new candidate starts out under a severe handicap in relation to the funds available to established and highly financed candidates.

Some of the billionaires for the 2012 and 2016 election are known: Rick Santorum was supported by the billionaire Foster Friess, Newt Gingrich was supported by casino magnate Sheldon Adelson, Scott Walker of Wisconsin is supported by the Koch brothers, Ted Cruz was supported by Robert Mercer, and Marco Rubio was supported by Norman Braman. Norman Braman, a Florida billionaire, is ready to invest $10 million or more to support Rubio's 2016 bid for the presidency. One can seriously ask whether these candidates can be free of influence when addressing legislation that might affect their supporters. We would assume that billionaire donors expect their candidates to behave in the donor's interests even if this collides with the public interest. We can ask what has happened to the 'one citizen, one vote' definition of democracy and whether we are living in a democracy or plutocracy.

WHAT PROPOSALS HAVE BEEN OFFERED TO CONTROL CAMPAIGN FINANCE?

The first question is whether any limits should be placed on how much a donor can spend on promoting a specific candidate. Assuming that it would be better to put donor limits on the size of their donation, what should that limit be?

The second question is whether to include corporations as persons and what amounts they can give. Some shareholders have objected to the money that their corporation is giving, and this adds to whether we can call a corporation a single person.

The third question is whether the names of all donors to political candidates should be made public. If the answer is yes, the amount donors give will go down, something not favored by most candidates. The basic question is whether citizens should know whose free speech is supporting whom.

The fourth question is whether controls can be put on the amount of 'soft' money that is supposed to help in social welfare causes but usually is tilted toward supporting one political party and candidates over others. There is a big blur between what is the free expression of ideas and the implied support for a particular political candidate. In November 2015, the *New York Times* reported that all of Senator Marco Rubio's $5.5 million pro-Rubio television ads were financed by secret donors through a tax-exempt 'social welfare' Super PAC that is not supposed to use money to support a particular candidate. Meanwhile the Internal Revenue Service and the Federal Election Commission have been silent on the matter.[17]

Here are the current rules for donor gifts to campaigns and candidates:

* A donor can give as much as $2,700 per candidate in that election cycle.
* A donor can give as much as $5,000 to a PAC per election cycle.
* A donor can give as much as $33,400 to a political party per year.
* A donor (individual or corporation) can give an unlimited amount to a Super PAC during that election cycle and the donor's name will not be public.
* A donor (individual or corporation) can give an unlimited amount to a social welfare organization and their name can remain private.

Clearly, rich donors and corporations have many ways to give lots of money to candidates and parties of their choice. Many proposals have been advanced for limiting the amount of political campaign expenditures. At one extreme would be to require all candidates to apply for public funds to finance their campaign, providing that they can raise a sufficient number of signatures supporting their candidacy. All candidates would receive the same amount to expend as they wish. They would also agree not to accept additional money from individual donors, corporations, unions, or nonprofit organizations.

The strongest advocate for other proposals is Lawrence Lessig, whose book is *Republic, Lost: How Money Corrupts Congress—and a Plan to Stop It*. Early on, Lessig called for a Constitutional Convention but later retreated as this idea came under attack. Then Lessig formed his own Super PAC called Mayday to raise funds to fight the other Super PACs. He used his Super PAC to support candidates who said that they would support campaign finance reform. He aimed to get his followers to support those candidates and talk against other candidates who would not support campaign finance reform.

Another concerned group, the Brennan Center for Justice, has proposed that the President issue an executive order requiring government contractors to disclose their campaign contributions. This would at least make their support public and hopefully lead to a reduction in political donations. The Brennan Center ultimately is hoping that the Supreme Court will extricate itself from viewing money as equal to free speech and undo *Citizens United*.

The 2010 *Citizens United* decision was, according to former president Jimmy Carter, 'the stupidest decision that the Supreme Court ever made.' He said that it turned America into an 'oligarchy' where power is wielded by wealthy elites. He said that it led to 'a complete subversion of our political system as a payoff to major contributors. The country is just an oligarchy with unlimited political bribery.' Carter said that the same applies to governors and U.S. Senators and Congress members. His condemnation has been echoed by Hillary Clinton and Supreme Court Justice Ruth Ginsburg.[18]

The proposal is to undo *Citizens United* and stop allowing corporations and unions to spend unlimited amounts of money on candidates and political parties. In addition, allow individual taxpayers to designate the first $200 of his or her taxes to support a political candidate. This would be a 'tax rebate for democracy' and send billions of small donations to favored political candidates who will no longer depend on high money interests for their election.[19]

Another proposal would be to restrict candidate political spending on TV and other media to a period of 30 days before the election. Britain, for example, compresses the electioneering period and believes that candidates can get their message across in a much shorter period of time. This would be much better than what is now taking place where candidates are involved in running from the end of the last election cycle over a whole two-year period.

Richard Painter wrote that even conservatives would benefit from limiting big money from influencing elections. He cited four reasons:

- Big money encourages big government, something that is anathema to conservatives. Campaign contributions lead to dreaming up wasteful programs—'bridges to nowhere, contracts for equipment the military does not need, solar energy companies that go bankrupt on the government's dime, and for-profit educational institutions that don't educate.'
- Campaign contributions lead to more regulation which conservatives hate. Regulated companies—banking, health care and energy—become the biggest contributors hoping their money would change regulations but these are rarely followed through. The politicians exploit these industries to get their money even though it doesn't lead to less regulation.
- Conservatives for other causes—anti-abortion, anti-gambling, anti-pornography—raise little money and their voice isn't heard because all the money and media direct attention to other issues.
- Big money also seeps in from foreign interests that find ways to support desired candidates. The American public is no longer the only party influencing the outcome of elections.[20]

DOES THE CANDIDATE WHO RECEIVED THE MOST POPULAR VOTES BECOME THE PRESIDENT?

We would think that in electing a President from the two leading candidates, the candidate with the most popular votes would become the President. Yet in four of our 57 presidential elections, the candidate with the most popular votes did not win:[21]

- In 1824, Andrew Jackson won the popular vote but got less than 50% of the electoral votes. John Quincy Adams became the next president when he was picked by the House of Representatives.
- In 1876, Samuel Tilden won the popular vote but lost the election when Rutherford B. Hayes got 185 electoral votes to Tilden's 184.
- In 1888, Grover Cleveland won the popular vote but lost the election when Benjamin Harrison got 233 electoral votes to Cleveland's 168.

- In 2000, Al Gore won the popular vote but lost the election to George Bush. In the most highly contested election in modern history, the U.S. Supreme Court stopped the Florida recount of ballots, giving Bush the state's 25 electoral votes for a total of 271 to Gore's 255.

The fact that the candidate who wins the most popular votes may not become the President can happen with the Electoral College voting system. Under the U.S. Constitution, the states have complete power to allocate their electoral votes. In several states, the state law calls for awarding all of a state's electoral votes to the candidate receiving the most popular votes in that state. That means the votes of those who voted against the most popular candidate in the state don't count.

Consider that Jeb Bush planned to win the presidency in 2016 by focusing mainly on two states, Florida and Ohio. Either could go Republican or Democratic and the winner would take all the votes. Bush could feel confident to win Florida because he was a past and respected Florida governor. To make sure he would win Ohio's votes, he would offer to pick John Kasich, the current Ohio governor, as his vice president running mate. However, he later got the news that John Kasich decided to go after the presidency himself.

A proposed bill called the National Popular Vote Bill calls for the presidency to be given to the presidential candidate who received the most popular votes in all 50 states (and the District of Columbia). This bill has already been enacted by 11 jurisdictions possessing 165 electoral votes—61% of the 270 electoral votes necessary to activate it. The bill would take effect when enacted by states possessing a majority of the electoral votes—that is, enough electoral votes to elect a President (270 of 538). Votes in the largest states would have a major influence on the presidential outcome. This also means that political candidates will spend most of their money and time promoting in our four largest states—California, Texas, New York, and Florida. When passed by a sufficient number of states, this bill would correct today's situation where candidates run most of their political campaigns in four states (Ohio, Florida, Virginia, and Iowa). Meanwhile they relatively ignore the 38 states that make much less of a difference in the outcome. The bill has passed in a total of 33 legislative chambers in 22 states. Once it is passed in a sufficient number of states, citizens can expect the President to always be the candidate who wins the most popular votes.[22] At the final national convention, instead of a state declaring that, 'the state of Oklahoma gives all of its votes to Mitt Romney,' the electors would state the number of votes they give to Mitt Romney and the number they give to Barack Obama. It actually would lead to the elimination of appointing Electors and the Electoral College.

IS THE WINNER-TAKES-ALL SYSTEM THE BEST WAY TO GET REPRESENTATIVE GOVERNMENT?

The system of electing Representatives and Senators is a 'winner-takes-all (WTA)' system. The candidates win who get a plurality majority of the votes in their single district. The alternative is a 'proportional representative (PR)' system. This has become the predominant voting system in 21 of 28 countries in Western Europe.

In the PR system, legislators are elected in multimember districts instead of single-member districts. The number of seats that a party will win in an election is proportional to the amount of its support among voters. Suppose the multimember district has ten member districts. If the Republicans win 50% of the votes, they will receive five of the ten seats. If Democrats win 40%, they will receive four seats. And if a third party wins 10% of the vote, they win one seat. There are a number of systems for implementing PR. PR voting systems tend to provide 'a more accurate representation of party strength, better representation for political and racial minorities, fewer wasted votes, higher levels of voter turnout, better representation of women, greater likelihood of majority rule, and little opportunity for gerrymandering.'[23]

WHAT SHOULD CONGRESS MEMBERS BE PAID?

The question arises whether members of Congress are being paid too much for their poor performance. Here are the current pay levels:

Salary of House/Senate members $174,000

Speaker of the House $223,500

Salary of Majority/Minority Leader $193,400

Compare this to:

Average salary of a teacher $40,065

Average salary of a deployed soldier $38,000

This led Warren Buffet and a group to propose a Congressional Reform Act in 2014:

- A Congressman/woman collects a salary while in office and receives no pay when they are out of office. No Tenure/No Pension.
- Congress participates in Social Security like all citizens.

- Congress can purchase their own retirement plan.
- Congress will no longer vote themselves a pay raise. Congressional pay will rise by the lower of CPI or 3%.
- Congress loses their current health care system and participates in the same health care system as the American people.
- Congress must equally abide by all law they impose on the American people.
- All contracts with past and present Congressmen/women are void effective December 31, 2014.

Serving in Congress is an honor, not a career. The point of this proposal is to stimulate fresh thinking by citizens about what they expect from members of Congress and how much reward they deserve for their service.

PROPOSALS FOR FIXING TERM LIMITS FOR MEMBERS OF CONGRESS

How long do members of Congress stay on the job? John Dingell of Michigan broke the House record at 59 years before he decided to retire. Robert Byrd of West Virginia broke the Senate record and lasted 51 years. Many Representatives and Senators spend over 30 and 40 years in Congress. The question arises: Are these long service periods good for the country? We have already put term limits on the U.S. presidency, limiting any president to two terms. The idea is to prevent a president from continuing indefinitely and either aggregating so much power or losing his mental or physical ability sometime in his long stay. We have not put term limits on Supreme Court members although most of them can easily accumulate 30 or 40 years on the Court. Maybe limiting Supreme Court justices to 30 years might be defended on concerns about senility or reduced physical energy.

One can offer strong arguments for putting term limits on members of Congress given their large number of years of incumbency and longevity:

1   Those Congress members with 30 or 40 years on the job may get out of touch with their newer constituency.
2   The same members may have built comfortable relations with many people from industry, agriculture, and the media and consciously or unconsciously give them more access and favor than would a new member of Congress.

It is probably a good idea to open political offices to fresh candidates from time to time. For the House, whose members need to be re-elected every two years, putting a ten-term limit gives the candidate 20 years to learn and do good for his or her country. For the Senate, whose members need to be re-elected every six years, limiting members to a four-term period allows them to be on the job for at least 24 years. There would be no prohibition for any Congress member to try on his or her last term to get elected to the other body of Congress. But most Congressional members are likely to end their final term with no regrets by joining a lobbyist firm and getting better pay than in Congress.

CONCLUSION

Many countries claim to be a democracy but few are full democracies. Just running elections is not enough to qualify as a democracy. The elections must be open and fair and free of threats, money payments, and other pressures.

Democracies work best when voters are well informed and determined to get to the ballot box and vote their interests. One hopes that the political candidates are highly qualified and will vote in the interests of their constituencies. Getting elected is a strenuous process that requires joining a political party, getting financial support from family, friends, and rich fans, and competing with others in the same party who seek the same office, and managing to get more votes than them.

Unfortunately, candidates cannot hope to win office without rich supporters. Candidates spend a great deal of their time before winning office and after winning office with their rich supporters. They lose in the process their independence in voting for the best interests of their constituency, especially if it dissatisfies their donors. The great and increasing role played by money in determining our leaders diminishes the quality of our democracy and its capability of serving and satisfying the interests of all our citizens.

NOTES

1   See: www.presidency.ucsb.edu/data/turnout.php (accessed 03.03.16).
2   See: E. Cepeda, 'Getting Hispanics to Vote', *New York Times*, April 5, 2015, p. 15A. Paul Taylor, 'The Growing Electoral Clout of Blacks Is Driven by Turnout, Not Demographics,' Pew Research Center, December 26, 2012.
3   See: Lexington, 'Not Running, but Fleeing', *The Economist*, May 16, 2015, p. 30.

4   N. Wolf, *Give Me Liberty: A Handbook for American Revolutionaries* (Simon & Schuster, New York, 2008), p. 344.

5   N. Kristoff, 'U.S.A., Land of Limitations?', *New York Times*, August 8, 2015.

6   For a most interesting history of the Voting Rights Act, see J. Ruttenberg, 'A Dream Undone: Inside the 50-year campaign to roll back the Voting Rights Act', *New York Times*, July 29, 2015.

7   N.Wolf, *Give Me Liberty*.

8   See: www.localelectors.org/2012/11/12/how-was-91-of-congress-re-elected-despite-a-10-approval-rating/ (accessed 03.03.16).

9   See: A. Lupia, *Uninformed: Why People Know So Little About Politics and What We Can Do About It* (Oxford University Press, Oxford, 2015).

10 A. MacGillis, 'Who Turned My Blue State Red? Why Poor Areas Vote for Politicians Who Want to Slash The Safety Net', *New York Times*, November 20, 2015.

11 N. Wolf, *Give Me Liberty*, pp. 345–347.

12 See: T. Amato and R. Nader, *Grand Illusion: The Fantasy of Voter Choice in a Two-Party Tyranny* (The New Press, New York, 2009).

13 F. X. Clines, 'All 17 Republican Candidates in One Place?', *New York Times*, July 15, 2015.

14 See: www.fixcapitalism.com, 'Move to Amend.' (accessed 03.03.16).

15 Adapted from Roger R. Berkowitz, 'A Brief History of Campaign Finance', February 9, 2012. (Hannah Arendt Center, Bard College:New York, 2012), www.hannaharendt center.org/?p=4247 (accessed 03.03.16).

16 E. Drew, 'How Money Runs Our Politics', *The New York Review*, June 4, 2015, pp. 22–26.

17 Editorial, 'Senator Rubio's Stealthy Donors', *New York Times*, November 23, 2015.

18 C. Burke, 'Jimmy Carter: "Unlimited Political Bribery" Subverts Nation', *Newsweek*, July 31, 2015.

19 R. W. Painter, 'Big Money, Big Government', *New York Times*, February 3, 2016.

20 Ibid.

21 See: www.history.com/topics/us-presidents/presidential-election-facts (accessed 03.03.16).

22 See: www.nationalpopularvote.com/pages/explanation.php. For more information, see FairVote.org. (accessed 03.03.16).

23 See: www.mtholyoke.edu/acad/polit/damy/BeginnningReading/PRsystems.htm (accessed 03.03.16).

CHAPTER 3

REFORMING CONGRESS—WHY DOES CONGRESS PERFORM POORLY?

'I have come to the conclusion that one useless man is a disgrace, that two become a law firm, and that three or more become a congress.'
John Adams

There is a long history of Americans being dissatisfied with Congress. Will Rogers once observed, 'I don't make jokes. I just watch the government and report the facts.' In a Gallup poll in 1973, Congress got a 42% public approval rating, its highest ever. On January 4, 2013, Congress scored last out of 16 institutions, with a 10% approval rating. In the summer of 2014, the rating fell to 7%.

A *New York Times*/CBS News Poll survey in February 2010 reported that 80% of Americans see Congress people as more interested in serving special interests than the people they represent. U.S. Representative Mark Pocan (Wisconsin) observed, 'Instead of being the world's greatest example of representative government, we seem to have become the nation's largest kindergarten—only with control of the nation's checkbook and nuclear arsenal.'

What drives our members of Congress? The nonpartisan Center on Congress surveyed participants during the 112th session of Congress (2011–2013) asking, 'What do you think is the main thing that influences what members of Congress do in office?' Of the participants, 49% chose the answer 'special interests', followed by 36% who said 'personal self-interest.' Only 14% believes that their representatives paid attention to what would be best for the people in their state, district, or country. If the U.S. was a parliamentary democracy instead of a presidential democracy, such a low vote of confidence would lead to a quick election to throw out the majority party and replace much of Congress with new members. But in a presidential system, instead of 90% of Congress members losing their jobs, 90% will still have their jobs and probably win in the next re-election period! Senator Tom Colburn observed, 'In several election cycles in recent history, more incumbents died in office than lost re-election bids.'

SETTING UP VOTING DISTRICTS

Today every one of the 50 states elects two Senators regardless of the state's size. California has only two Senators and so does Rhode Island, in spite of their great difference in size. On the other hand, the voters in each state elect a number of House Representatives reflecting the size of that state. California sends 53 Congress members to the House of Representatives and Rhode Island sends only two Congress members to the House.

Today the House of Representatives contains 435 members. Each member represents a district that averages about 700,000 people. Some have argued that it is hard for a House member to know much about the interests of 700,000 people, but to have a smaller population making up a district would require many more districts and Representatives. Congress favors keeping the number of Congressional districts at 435.

The framers of the Constitution state that the size of Congressional districts should be as equal as possible. Individual states can lay down rules such as stating that the difference between the largest and smallest district in the state cannot vary by more than 10%, for example. The underlying purpose is to get as close as possible to equalizing the voting influence of each Representative and therefore of each citizen.

In earlier times, the voting population was defined as male citizens at the age of 21 and over. Later the population count became based on the number of male and female citizens. Still later each state could decide on the minimum voting age with 18 being the preferred age although 16 or 17 is specified in some states. New issues have arisen about how to define the eligible voting population. Does it include the native Indian population, the prison population, or the ex-offender population? The Democratic Party favors defining the population number as large as possible because more voters of the usually excluded populations are likely to vote as Democrats. This issue is likely to be taken up by the Supreme Court.

GERRYMANDERING AFFECTS THE SIZE AND SHAPE OF VOTING DISTRICTS

There are 435 voting districts in the U.S.. Some estimate that only 15 of the 435 Houses seats will be truly contested in 2016. What accounts for the high retention rate of incumbents? One explanation is that incumbents benefit from having redesigned their voting district, with the help of their legislature, to contain most of their supporters. For example, many Democrats live in central cities and many Republicans live in suburbs. So, an elected Republican would like the district to only include the suburbs; and an elected Democrat would like the district to consist of the whole city. President Obama said gerrymandering is one of the fundamental problems in American politics: 'I think we've got to end the practice of drawing our congressional districts so that politicians can pick their voters, and not the other way around…Let a bipartisan group do it.'[1]

Gerrymandering is the name given to this redrawing of political boundaries in order to give a party or candidate a numeric advantage over an opposing party or candidate. The original voting district might be fairly circular or square and later be redrawn by a certain group in the legislature so that it aggregates more of a party's voters into the redrawn voting district. The new voting district might look more like a salamander than a circle or square. In a 5-to-2 decision in 2015, the Florida Supreme Court ruled that a 2012 redistricting map drawn by the Republican-led legislature had been tainted by 'unconstitutional intent to favor the Republican Party and incumbent lawmakers,' and that Republican 'operatives' and political consultants 'did in fact conspire to manipulate and influence the redistricting process.'[2]

Congressional redistricting has become a rigged political game by different parties at different times. Normally the leading party politicians want to reserve the right to draw the redistricting map. They will redraw the map to favor their incumbents. The incumbents become more secure in their seats. They can stick closely to their party and their donors. They have less incentive to compromise. They can please the most extreme elements in their party and not worry. The result: the two parties become more polarized.

Increasingly, citizens are calling for an independent redistricting commission to redraw the map. There are now 14 states that allow initiative referendums introduced by citizens through a petition process either to the legislature or directly to the voters with an additional eight states that allow indirect initiatives. Nonpartisan committees or computer programs should redraw the state maps for congressional seats (state and local) after each ten-year census. Commissions in Arizona, Florida, and California now invite citizens instead of self-interested politicians in the legislature to draw alternative maps. They will encourage the drawing to be as close as possible to a dense circle or square. But legislators in Arizona sued to be put back in charge and this case went before the Supreme Court. The Supreme Court, in a 5–4 vote, ruled in favor of independent commissions and other means of drawing up voting districts instead of leaving it only to Congress or state legislatures. The decision says that partisan gerrymandering is incompatible with democratic principles and that the people should be the originating source of all the powers of government.

Incumbents are likely to be re-elected for other reasons. Incumbents are able to raise more money, mount a stronger campaign, and have better name recognition. Another factor is that voters first get to choose candidates in primary elections but only 15.9% of all eligible citizens participated in the 2012 statewide primary elections (according to the Bipartisan Policy Center): 'The few people who do vote in the primaries tend to be members of special interest groups that the incumbents have worked hard to turn into supporters.' They are likely to receive political favors for voting for them. Others might assume that the incumbents have accumulated on-the-job experience, which makes them more effective than the challengers. In a general election, the choice boils down to voting either for the Democrats or Republicans. Two-thirds of the voters vote for their favorite party.

The economist Paul Krugman distinguishes between the actual primary and what precedes it, the 'invisible primary.' Candidates must first compete for winning the support of crucial elites. These elites used to be the political establishment and opinion leaders but now it is about winning support from a few dozen plutocrats. To quote Krugman, 'the GOP [the Republican Party] is on track to nominate someone who has won over the big money by promising government by the 1%, for the 1%.'[3]

DOES CONGRESS KNOW WHAT AMERICAN CITIZENS REALLY WANT?

The U.S. Congress consists of 535 members—435 Representatives and 100 Senators—who were elected to represent the will of the country's citizens who are registered to vote, namely 146,311,000 citizens. It is hard to believe that 535 people can know enough about the wishes and interests of 146,311,000 citizens. Yet elected Republicans always say they know what American citizens want. And elected Democrats say they know what American citizens want. The only problem is that they present two different theories of what American citizens want.

The only real way to find out what American citizens want is to create a huge carefully worded questionnaire listing dozens of issues and asking registered American citizens to state their preferences. All the questions would be worded with a simple 'Yes' or 'No' answer. Consider the following sample questions:

- Do you believe that men and women should receive equal pay for equal work?
- Do you believe that a pregnant woman has the right to determine whether she will have an abortion?
- Do you believe that persons who are now in the U.S. but who entered the U.S. illegally, should be able to go through a process of becoming a citizen?

The answers to these questions would give legislators hard information on voter preferences. At the same time, any Representative would have the right to go against the whole U.S. vote if his or her district consists of voters with a different preference. It may be that 70% of U.S. voters favor equal gender pay for equal work, but the voters in Mississippi, or some city in Mississippi, may be largely against equal pay for equal work. The whole point of dividing the U.S. into districts is to have the elected Representative vote for what the citizens in that district favor. That is why there are so many polls rather than one poll for the whole nation.

The good news is that local and state polls can help legislators determine the will of the majority. The bad news is that many polls are rigged—worded in such a way to get the answers a politician or party wants to get. Politicians of opposing parties will cite the specific polls that favor their political philosophy. That is why a lot of citizens are not overly impressed with poll findings.

The fact is that most politicians personally meet only a very small fraction of the citizens they represent. Even if they call for live public gatherings to discuss an important issue, only a fraction of the concerned voters shows up, often an unrepresentative fraction consisting of the citizens who have more time on their hands or who want to agitate for a position. The root problem is that any legislator has only a poor and often distorted picture of what voters in their district might want.

In this chapter on Reforming Congress, we will consider three issues:

- What is the structure of Congress?
- How does the legislative process work?
- What problems need fixing in the legislative process?

WHAT IS THE STRUCTURE OF CONGRESS?

The U.S. Congress is a bicameral legislative body, with the House chamber elected from the states in proportion to the state's population, and the Senate chamber containing two Senators from each of the 50 states.

Each of the 535 legislators will have a budget and staff to carry on much of the work of reading bills, assessing what the citizens in that district want, listening to lobbyists and other interested parties, and advising the legislature on the best course of action. Each legislator will be on one or more committees, such as foreign policy, education, health, armed forces, and so on. Each committee is headed by a chairperson from the winning party who has the power to influence the shape of the bill and to slow down or expedite a bill's movement toward a final vote.

Legislators differ in how long they have been in Congress. The power and the most important committees will be in the hands of the most senior legislators. Junior legislators are wise to defer to the opinion of senior legislators if they want to advance smoothly in the system. Each party will have a leader in the House and the Senate. In 2015, the Republicans were the House Majority. Representative John Boehner was the Speaker of the House and he had several roles: He is the presiding officer and administrative head of the House, the leader of the Republican Party, and an elected Representative of the House. The Speaker of the House is next in line to succeed the President and the Vice President if necessary. In addition to the Speaker, the Republicans have a Majority Whip who assists in managing the party's legislative program; a Republican Conference Chairman who heads the organization of all Republican Party members of the House; and a Republican Policy Committee Chairman who heads the Conference forum for policy development. The minority Democratic Party has similar positions of leadership. The current Senate is headed by the Senate Majority Leader, Senator Mitch McConnell. In addition, there is a Republican Conference Chair, Republican Policy Committee Chair, and a Republican Conference Vice-Chair. The Democratic Party in the Senate has similar Chairs.

HOW DOES THE LEGISLATIVE PROCESS WORK?

Mark Twain showed his skepticism about the legislative process when he said, 'No man's life, liberty, or property is safe while the legislature is in session.' Yet the legislative process must take place. One or more legislators will develop a bill in either the House or Senate to meet some real or perceived needs of the citizens. The bill will be sent to the appropriate committee that will suggest or undertake modifications of the bill and either approve it going further, dismiss it, or delay it. The committee may add other items to the bill, subtract some items, or make other modifications in the interest of raising the probability of its passage. The bill will be sent to the other chamber to consider and there it may undergo further modification. The bill may pass back and forth between the House and Senate until it is ready to be voted on in each chamber. Usually the bill can be passed with a majority vote. If passed, it then goes to the President (or Governor or Mayor) for his or her signature. The Executive has the right to veto the bill and send it back to the legislature, which can override the Executive's veto if two-thirds of the legislatures support it a second time.

Most of the work of the House and Senate is done by committees that craft legislation, oversee executive agencies, and formulate, and oversee, national policy. Congressional committees fall into four broad categories: standing, select, special and joint.

Standing committees are permanent bodies and act as the workhorses of Congress. They conduct hearings and investigations and oversee legislation and federal agencies within their jurisdiction. Examples of standing committees are the House and Senate committees on agriculture, appropriations, armed services, financial institutions (banking), commerce, and foreign relations.

Select committees and *special committees* are temporary committees created for a special purpose, often investigative, and may be dissolved once that purpose is completed. Select committees may span several Congresses while special committees may fall within the two-year span of a Congress. These committees may hold hearings and issue reports, but they don't report on legislation. Among them are the Senate Special Committee on Aging, the Committee on Ethics, and the Senate Select Committee on Intelligence.

Joint committees may be temporary or permanent bodies, and their defining characteristic is a membership composed of equal numbers of Representatives and Senators. Among them are the Joint Tax Committee and the Joint Economic Committee. These joint committees as viewed as instruments for fostering collaboration between the House and the Senate.

Background to Congressional Committees

Committees are the major workhorses in the legislature. They are defined by their history and jurisdiction, chairmanships, numbers of assignments per member, staffing and party ratios in determining committee makeup. In 1946, a Legislative Reorganization Act was enacted to reduce the number of committees from 33 to 15 in the Senate and from 48 to 19 in the House. Many

(Continued)

(Continued)

standing committees were changed into subcommittees, which greatly enhanced the power of the remaining chairmen. The 1946 Act also authorized committees to hire as many as four professional and six clerical employees, thus providing committees greater expertise in handling complicated policy issues. The Act required committees to hold open public hearings where possible and to keep accurate records.

The Legislative Reorganization Act succeeded in reducing the number of full committees, but it failed to limit the number of subcommittees. The result was an explosion of subcommittees. Where there were in 1949 only 60 subcommittees in the House and an equal number in the Senate, by 1975 the number had jumped to over 145 in the House and about 120 in the Senate. This led to junior members having subcommittee chairmanships which eroded the power of the older and more conservative full committee chairmen. The authority of full committee chairmen diminished with the shift of power to subcommittees.

The Legislative Reorganization Act of 1970 increased the number of permanent professional staffers to six per standing committee, allowing committees to seek additional technical and scientific personnel and to request funding for temporary staff. The 1970 Act also required that one-third of funding for staff be directed to the minority party, and gave the minority the right to call witnesses at hearings. The Act required committees to have written rules of procedure, that roll call votes be placed on the public record, and that committee reports on bills be made available for inspection three or more days before that legislation could be considered on the floor. It also allowed House committee proceedings to be broadcast by radio or television.

In the 1970s, the Senate adopted a 'subcommittee bill of rights,' allowing subcommittees to choose their own chairmen, develop subcommittee budgets, and require committee chairmen to refer legislation to the appropriate subcommittee within two weeks of referral to the full committee. Subcommittees could set their own meeting and hearing dates. Committees could now staff to 18 professional and 12 clerical workers, and one-third of committee staff was reserved for the minority.

Congress also needed to centralize its own budgeting process. A joint budget committee would draft an annual budget containing estimates of revenues and expenditures and setting appropriations limits for each agency. If estimated revenues were exceeded, a debt ceiling would be established. Congress would add specific spending prohibitions to the text of appropriations bills in order to show fiscal restraint.

In the 1980s and 1990s, several more changes occurred, including an effort to reduce the number of subcommittees and increase the power of the full committees. The names of many standing committees were changed, and both chambers passed a series of ethics rules affecting honoraria, outside income, and post-employment lobbying.

In the 1990s, party leaders began to assert more control over subcommittee and full committee chairmen in favor of policies advanced by leadership task forces. The Republican Party task forces often moved initiatives to the floor without committee referral. This is more like a parliamentary system in which the majority party moves key legislation without standing committees or involving the minority party in the legislative process.

Despite the history of rules and procedures to refer everything to committees, majority party leaders are learning to work around the process and bring bills directly to the House floor, bypassing some of the technical resources found in committees. A tension clearly exists between party government and the committee system. Party government diminishes the participation of the minority party, reduces the influence of committee chairmen, moves decision making outside the committee system and behind closed doors, and makes it more difficult to align deliberation by the two chambers. On the other hand, it has the advantage of speeding up action on major initiatives. We will have to see in the future whether government by party will continue or government by committee will make a comeback in federal legislative matters.[4]

WHAT PROBLEMS NEED FIXING IN THE LEGISLATIVE PROCESS?

Here we examine several practices occurring during the legislative process that draw widespread criticism and may warrant correction.

ADDING AN UNWANTED OR IRRELEVANT PROVISION TO A BILL UNDER CONSIDERATION

One political party may attach an unwelcome provision to a bill that the other party wants to pass. If the party favoring the bill passes it, it will have to live with the undesired addition stuck into the bill.

As an example, Senate Democrats wanted to pass a bill that would thwart human trafficking. However, Republicans added an unwanted provision that increased the number of anti-abortion restrictions. Democratic Senator Chuck Schumer noted, 'They're putting poison pills in their own bills.' The Senate Democrats reluctantly voted down the bill that they wanted which would have reduced sex trafficking. In resentment, Republican Senate Majority Leader Mitch McConnell indicated he would delay President Obama's Loretta Lynch nomination to be Attorney General. Loretta Lynch would have been the first black woman to serve in this position and she is highly qualified. Yet Lynch's confirmation was held up longer than any other nomination for attorney general in the last three decades.

The solution? One hopes that Congress can agree to draft and pass bills to which no irrelevant provisions can be added. Both parties would gain in the long run, Congress would legislate more speedily, and the public would be served much better.

EARMARKING

Earmarking is a process by which a congressional expenditure of funds is specified to apply to a particular project.

For example, in 2005, a $223 million earmark was passed to fund the construction of a bridge from Ketchikan, Alaska, to the tiny island of Gravina, Alaska. This was to satisfy a certain Congressman who wanted to look good to some citizens in his district. It was added to a bill funding reconstruction following Hurricane Katrina, which has nothing to do with Alaska. This earmark drew so much scorn that Congress stripped the earmark.

When Republicans took control of the House in 2011, they eliminated earmarks altogether in the name of good government. But today some oppose this ban on earmarks, saying that it amounts to leaving bureaucrats in the Executive Branch to determine where appropriations should go and this will be less transparent to voters than leaving it to Congress.

PORK BARREL

Pork barreling is the idea that Congress has a lot of money to appropriate and they might as well take some of the money to burnish favorite projects of their own. The idea is that there is a lot of 'pork' to share. Maxwell Anderson's play of 1933 about Congress called *Both Your Houses* won the Pulitzer Prize for exposing Congressional sessions where the lawmakers get more interested in supporting personal or lobbied business projects than serving the national interest. Very often lawmakers will agree to vote for other lawmakers' bills in exchange for votes on their bills.

The good news is that President Clinton in 1996 managed to sign into law a bill authorizing a line-item veto which can be used to fight 'special-interest boondoggles, tax loopholes and pure pork.' The President could cut down waste, protect taxpayers, and balance the budget better. Clinton noted that governors in 43 of the 50 states also had some type of line-item veto powers.[5]

For nearly three decades, each year Congress took up a 'tax extenders package' with more than 50 tax breaks affecting specific industries and issues. Many items amount to handing out 'corporate welfare.' One item may allow Hollywood producers to deduct up to $20 million for shooting films in specific locations; another item allows owners of racehorses to depreciate their prize animals over three years. The public would find it hard to know the true costs of these corporate handouts. Many people would like to see an ending to the annual tax extenders package.[6]

FILIBUSTER

One or more members of Congress may be anxious to stop a measure from being voted on or going through further debate. This tactic is called a filibuster. It came from the Spanish word *filibustero* to describe pirates that plundered in the 17th Century.

On June 26, 2013, Texas Democratic Senator Wendy Davis gave a non-stop 13-hour speech to prevent passage of an anti-abortion bill by reading from a binder filled with stories of women affected by the anti-abortion issue. Under Texas' Senate rules, Davis was not allowed to sit, lean against a desk, eat, drink, go to the restroom, or talk about anything unrelated to Senate Bill 5 during this time. Not to be outdone, on September 25, 2014, Republican Senator Ted Cruz filibustered for 21 hours with anti-Obamacare talk mixed with Dr. Seuss and Star Wars and other irrelevant references.

There is no doubt that filibusters lead to Congressional paralysis and dysfunction often to satisfy only one or a few passionate opponents. In 2005, President Obama had called for 'the elimination of the routine use of the filibuster in the Senate.' At a time like today when both parties are gridlocked, filibustering tends to occur more frequently. In the year 2013–2014, 218 times votes were held to end filibusters. The original purpose of the filibuster was to permit minorities or minor views to be heard, but today it is used by the major parties to stop the other party from advancing its platform. Filibustering, when it amounts to reading the telephone directory or nursery rhymes, has nothing to do with advancing debate on the measures.

The Senate filibuster rule has no Constitutional basis. Each house of Congress can determine its own procedural rules under the Constitution. It came up because the Senate refused to impose constraints on how long Senators may speak on a particular matter. The Senate did establish that a filibuster could be closed on a motion requiring 60 Senators to pass and end delaying tactics. The House has a different rule. In November 2013, the House in a majority vote abolished the filibuster for presidential appointees and judicial nominees below the Supreme Court.

Clearly, Congress should do more to limit or discipline the practice of filibustering. The filibuster should use the time to advance his or her arguments against the opposition. A time limit of a couple of hours should be set that is long enough for any proponent or opponent of a bill to share his or her basic position. A numerical limit should also be set on how many proponents and opponents of a bill can speak. Without such limits, everyone opposed to a bill will try to use the maximum time to essentially repeat each other's arguments.

SHUTTING DOWN THE GOVERNMENT

In October 2013, the U.S. federal government suffered a costly shutdown that lasted from October 1 to October 16, 2013. The shutdown occurred because Congress could not agree to legislation appropriating funds for fiscal year 2014. As a result, 800,000 federal employees were indefinitely furloughed and 1.3 million were required to report to work without known payment dates. This 16-day-long October 2013 shutdown was the third-longest in U.S. history, after the 18-day shutdown in 1978 and the 21-day 1995–96 shutdown.[7]

As background, the Republican-led House of Representatives attempted to delay or defund the Affordable Care Act ('Obamacare'). The House and Senate could not agree by September 30, 2013 and the federal government had to shut down on October 1 due to a lack of appropriated funds at the start of the new 2014 federal fiscal year. Yet many aspects of the Affordable Care Act were nevertheless implemented, starting on October 1, 2013. Finally, late in the evening of October 16, 2013, Congress passed the Continuing Appropriations Act 2014. The President signed it shortly after midnight on October 17, ending the government shutdown.

There is real damage caused by federal government shutdowns and it shakes public confidence in the party causing it and in Congress as a whole. Another government shutdown almost occurred in November 2015 instigated by Senator Ted Cruz and other Republicans, but fortunately it was averted. It would be better for all concerned if a measure could be passed preventing any future government shutdowns from occurring and forcing the parties to resolve their disputes in another way.

NOT PROVIDING ENOUGH MONEY FOR ENFORCEMENT

Congress may finally pass a piece of legislation but fail to provide enough money for its enforcement. It could claim to citizens that it has responded to their interests but in fact it would not have delivered on its promise.

As an example, in 2011, Congress enacted a farsighted food safety reform law. Thousands of people had been sickened by tainted products such as peanut butter, eggs, spinach, and melons. The Center for Disease Control and Prevention (CDC) estimated that 1 in 6 Americans got sick, 128,000 were hospitalized and 3,000 died of food-borne sicknesses. The Congressional Budget Office estimated that the Food and Drug Administration (FDA) would need $580 million from 2011 to 2015 to reform food programs in the U.S. Even this was considered a paltry sum in the vast federal budget. Yet Congress agreed to less than half of this amount. In this way the reforms symbolically looked serious but in fact lacked substance.[8]

THE POWER OF THE HOUSE RULES COMMITTEE

Whereas the Senate permits unlimited discussion or debate on a bill, the House tends to limit debate and uses its Rules Committee. This Rules Committee determines under what *rule* other bills will come to the floor. When a bill is reported out of a House committee, it does not go straight to the House floor. It is placed on the appropriate House Calendar for debate. The Rules Committee decides for how long and under what rules the full body will debate the proposition. The Committee might limit the number or types of amendments and may even allow no amendments. The Committee determines the amount of speaking time assigned on each bill or resolution, including no speaking time in some cases. Clearly, the Rules Committee exercises a powerful influence in the House. The same can happen in the Senate. Many bills get delayed, buried, or dropped.

As an example, Senator Elizabeth Warren asked for a unanimous consent to vote on her bill: The Bank on Students Emergency Loan Refinancing Act. This bill would allow more than 25 million people to refinance their student loans to today's lower 4% interest rates. But Senate Republicans blocked her bill because it would raise taxes on the wealthy. Republican Senator John Cornyn wanted the bill to be subject to amendments but Warren would not agree to unlimited amendments. Lawmakers in the end refused to take a vote on the grounds that they needed to focus on a more immediate stopgap spending measure to fund the government.[9]

Another way to get Congress to act is for citizens to call for referendums. There are 25 states that allow popular referendums by which voters may petition to demand popular votes on new laws by the legislature.

WHAT EXTERNAL INFLUENCES AFFECT THE BILLS THAT ARE PASSED?

Here we need to examine the role of two problems that affect the integrity of the members of Congress. The first is influence of lobbyists on their decision making. The second is the occurrence of outright corruption.

THE INFLUENCE OF LOBBYISTS

Lobbying describes the effort of organizations and their representatives (called lobbyists) to influence decisions made by government officials such as legislators, regulators, or judges. The term comes from the fact that 'influence peddlers' would appear in the lobbies of legislative buildings to 'buttonhole' legislators and influence their voting on behalf of the lobbyist's clients. Most of the lobbyists are lawyers and many are ex-members of Congress. Some say that they constitute the 'fourth branch' of government. Lobbying takes place at every level of government—federal, state, county, municipal, and local governments.

In 1971, there were only 175 registered lobbying firms; in 2012, there were over 13,700 registered lobbyists spending more than $3.3 billion annually in Washington, D.C. to influence legislators. General Electric alone spent $21.4 million, and Google came in second and spent $18.2 million. This doesn't account for non-registered lobbyists bearing the names 'government relations,' 'public affairs,' and 'corporate communications.' In addition, there are many business-funded think-tanks providing information often of a persuasive character. And we are not citing all the lobbying going on in U.S. states and cities.[10]

A large American company may use ten or more full-time registered lobbyists from several lobbying firms. It can also call on the services of retired politicians who are now lobbyists to assist when a big issue is at stake. Lobbyists used to lobby mainly to prevent tax increases or new regulations, then they moved to lobby for better roads and infrastructure and then they moved to press for company or industry specific benefits.[11]

An example of the power of lobbyists is the 2015 completion of General Dynamics' $3.3 billion Zumwalt destroyer. The U.S. has the largest and most powerful Navy in the world and yet it continues to build new ships. Navy ship builders influence the Navy Secretary, Ray Mabus, to tell a House Appropriations Committee that the Navy must get bigger, to move from 275 ships to a total of at least 300 ships. Governor Bobby Jindal of Louisiana told the American Enterprise Institution that if cuts were made to the defense budget, 'America will not have a global Navy any more.' Politicians are ready to serve the interests of business rather than provide badly needed money to help U.S. kids get a better education.[12]

The charge is made by Senator Elizabeth Warren and other progressive Democrats that Business runs the country, not Congress. How have big banks such as Citicorp and JPMorgan got away without any punishment for the role that they played in selling junk investment grade securities to the rest of the world? How come so many U.S. industries have achieved special treatment by Congress? Why doesn't Congress help citizens achieve lower drug prices from large pharmaceutical companies, something that happens in Canada and Europe? Why is the sugar industry receiving continuous protection even though their sugar prices are much higher than the cost of imported sugar from abroad?[13] While Republicans continually attack consumer benefit legislation and agencies, why don't they also attack the rampant level of 'corporate welfare-ism?'

Do politically active corporations get a good return on the money they give to lobbyists to achieve business favors and support? One study in 2014 showed that the 200 most politically active corporations spent $5.8 billion on federal lobbying and campaign contributions and got a hefty return of 4.4 trillion.[14] Professor John Friedman in another study estimated that pharmaceutical firms spent $130 million to help pass the Medicare Modernization Act of 2003 and this gave the industry a healthy return of $242 billion over a ten-year period following the Act's passage. Lee Drutman of the New American Foundation think-tank showed that the more companies lobby, the lower their effective tax rate, and that lobbying firms are less likely to be detected for fraud.[15]

There is evidence that once companies start lobbying, they continue it; lobbying has stickiness. There is also evidence that lobbying begets more lobbying, and the industry will keep growing.

VIEWS ABOUT LOBBYING

Many view lobbying activities as bad in leading elected officials to vote in favor of the lobbyists' clients—corporations and wealthy families rather than the public interest. Francis Fukuyama labeled the U.S. system of government a 'vetocracy' bordering on 'interest group capitalism.'[16] He sees the lobbyists as representing a multitude of interest groups that dominate and direct the legislators on how to vote, making the executives (the President, governors, and mayors) fairly impotent. In directing the elected officials to attend to business' interests, they distract interest in the real issues affecting the future of the country.

In the 'bad' category are the lobbyists for certain major industries, such as the oil industry, agriculture industry, pharmaceutical industry, and the defense industry. Lobbyists for the oil industry have managed to get strong government subsidies and privileges for that industry. Lobbyists for the agriculture industry basically serve the corporate owners of vast agricultural land rather than the small farmers. Lobbyists for the pharmaceutical industry have helped support high U.S. drug prices by keeping out foreign drugs and delaying generic drugs. Lobbyists for the defense industry keep legislators actively voting for more military goods even when the military generals don't need or want them.

Lobbyists undoubtedly influence the voting decisions of elected officials. Each legislator faces a mounting cost to get elected or re-elected way beyond his or her personal income and the income of friends and acquaintances. Each legislator needs campaign donations beyond what the political party can supply. Lobbyists are able to direct campaign donations coming from their client corporations. Lobbyists cannot explicitly ask for the legislator's vote in return for a campaign donation. But clearly, legislators know that their vote will have an effect on the size of donor support. Legislators know that voting favorably for the interests of certain companies will also increase chances to become a lobbyist after the legislator's career is over. Fully half of all Congress members become lobbyists after leaving office. A member of Congress can make several times his or her former annual salary of $187,000 by becoming a lobbyist.

Raising enough campaign finance money is a cancer that gets legislators to focus more on the interests of big corporations and wealthy families than on what best serves the interests of the voters in their district. Here is how Richard Wolff sees the relationship between Big Politics and Big Wealth:

> A rather vicious cycle has been at work for years. Reduced taxes on the rich leave them with more money to influence politicians and politics. Their influence wins them further tax reductions, which gives them still more money to put to political use. When the loss of tax revenue from the rich worsens already strained government budgets, the rich press politicians to cut public services and government jobs and not even debate a return to the higher taxes the rich used to pay. So it goes…[17]

We must recognize that lobbying is essentially a marketing activity. The wealthy company or family hires a lobbyist with an issue in mind. The lobbyist identifies the relevant key legislators to approach and develops the right arguments, communication and persuasion strategy. Lobbyists aim to develop a close and trusting relationship with various legislators and supply them with helpful information. Lobbyists must not commit the error of feeding dishonest facts to the legislator and thereby embarrassing the legislator, who will never again listen to that lobbyist. Although the facts are usually correct, the lobbyist puts them into a context that favors voting a certain way.

Lobbyists say that they don't approach a legislator and offer a political contribution if the legislator will vote a certain way. Often it is the legislator who phones a lobbyist and asks for a political contribution, sometimes even stating the amount. Elected officials today spend countless hours on the phone to raise money for their campaigns. The real story here is not one of lobbyists corrupting honest policymakers, but one of elected officials hitting on lobbyists in what resembles legalized extortion.

Lobbyists are paid a salary and are given a budget to cover expenses and also contributions to legislators' campaigns. Lawrence Lessig has published one of the most damaging indictments of lobbying in his *Republic, Lost: How Money Corrupts Congress—and a Plan to Stop It*.[18] The Supreme Court decision in *Citizens United* ended up declaring that businesses were persons with a right to influence other citizens. The result is that more Americans see special interests funnel huge amounts of business money into influencing Congress. Wall Street manages Congress rather than Congress managing Wall Street. Although there is little evidence of overt bribery, a lobbyist implied statement such as 'If you aren't able to vote for X, I'll have to contribute $1,000,000 to your opponent' is likely to have a strong effect.

Can corruption be taking place even when bribery doesn't take place? Campaign contributions are clearly illegal if there is an explicit *quid pro quo*. In the absence of an explicit *quid pro quo*, campaign contributions are legal. But today legislators spend half their time seeking and responding to funders of their campaigns and keeping them happy. Doesn't this corrupt the legislators and make them vote in the interests of the funders as opposed to the public? We should reject or limit the private financing of political campaigns. We should ban corporate funding of political campaigns and limit total campaign spending to the extent possible.[19]

Does lobbying activity really pay off? Some studies have tried to show that many legislators are not overly influenced by campaign contributions. But Lessig shows that elected officials can influence legislation in other ways such as by delaying or modifying certain bills or voting them down. He shows how legislators adjust their views in advance before asking for contributions, so there is no explicit evidence of a change in a legislator's view as a result of asking for contributions.

Other studies indicate that lobbying has a great impact on Congressional bills and policy making. A 2011 meta-analysis of research findings found a positive correlation between corporate political activity and corporate performance.[20] A 2009 study found that lobbying brought a substantial return on investment, as much as 22,000% in some cases.[21]

However, we need to acknowledge instances of 'good lobbying' by groups trying to counter the misstatements and misinformation of other lobbyists, as well as represent advocacy groups such as environmental, educational, and health care groups. For example, the American Medical Association lobbied Congress to pass laws against tobacco advertising or sales to minors. Most citizens would consider this to be a good lobbying effort.

THE RELATED PROBLEM OF 'DARK MONEY' AND BUYING ELECTIONS

In addition to the lobbying problem of influencing legislators, there is the problem of buying political elections. In his State of the Union address, President Obama said, 'The secret billionaire and big business "dark money" is pulling our politics into the gutter.' 'Dark money' describes money spent to influence political election outcomes where there is no disclosure of the donors. Are the donors only rich Americans or could they even be foreign donors who are influencing our elections? In 2006, only $5.2 million came from organizations that did not disclose donors. By 2012, over $300 million came from tax-exempt organizations. The 2016 election will substantially exceed the 2012 election level of dark money.

The Supreme Court's 2010 *Citizens United* decision led to the set up of PACs and Super PACs. PACs involve money donated to social welfare nonprofit organizations. The PACs do not have to disclose who gave the money. PACs must be 'operated exclusively to promote social welfare.' Political activity is allowed but must not be the organization's 'primary' mission. The current IRS commissioner said that groups could spend up to 49% of revenues on political activity and still keep their tax exemption. Many PACs do spend under 49% for political activity. Even the nonpolitical part usually takes the form of issue ads where no candidate is mentioned but it is very clear what candidate favors that issue. It is outrageous that tax-exempt organizations can spend so much on political activity when the purpose of these organizations is primarily to promote social welfare.[22]

The Super PACs are similar to traditional PACs that can raise and spend money but they do have to report the names of their donors. They can raise unlimited amounts of money from corporations, unions, individuals, and associations. They can advocate for the election or defeat of candidates for federal office by purchasing television, radio, and print advertisements and other media. There are both conservative and liberal Super PACs.

PROPOSED SOLUTIONS TO THE LOBBYING PROBLEM

Clearly, governments must pass laws regulating the influence of lobbyists. Lobbyists' activities must be reported and be free of overt bribery. Lobbying is subject to extensive rules that, if not followed, can lead to penalties including jail. Yet the activity of lobbying is legal and is interpreted by court rulings as free speech and is protected by the US Constitution. Among the solutions proposed to limit lobbying are:

1 A cooling-off period that makes congressional staff and others wishing to enter the lobbying field wait a year or more before they can become a lobbyist.
2 Requiring lobbyists to register. Requiring them to report contacts and expenditures. Reporting which businesses and organizations lobby, how, to whom, and for how much.
3 Establishing a ban on personal gifts.
4 Putting limits on campaign contribution amounts.
5 Requiring political candidates to voluntarily agree to take only small ($100 max) contributions.
6 Allowing federal tax payers to check off a certain amount to go to specific Congressional candidates.

THE INFLUENCE OF CORRUPTION

In any citizen-oriented political system, the rule needs to be that elected officials are honor-bound to represent the public interest. Elected officials are not to use their power to serve the special interests of friends, family, and other acquaintances when it is not in the public interest. Elected officials can listen to the needs and appeals of corporations, unions, and other associations but not be in their 'pocket' when it comes to vote-counting. Unfortunately, many members of Congress are clearly in the 'pocket' of certain groups such as the gun lobby, the cigarette lobby, the oil lobby, the pharmaceutical lobby, and other interest groups. Elected officials can favor certain groups but must not accept money or favors in deciding how to vote.

A respected and independent group called CREW (Citizens for Responsibility and Ethics in Washington) is active in identifying any voting behavior by public officials that could be induced by corrupt means. In 2013, CREW listed 13 House Representatives (nine Republicans and four Democrats) as the most corrupt members of Congress.

Charges of political corruption have occurred regularly in American history against specific Congress members, governors, and mayors, and various legislators in states and cities. Of Illinois' last seven governors, four have ended up going to prison on charges varying from racketeering, bribery, or bank fraud.

My guess, however, is that over 99% of our public officials are lawful and careful. Professor Stephen Medvic says that the U.S. Department of Justice prosecutes about 900 public officials for corruption each year. And only a fraction of them are elected officials. This is a very small percentage of the more than 500,000 elected officials in the U.S.[23]

In 2007, the Senate passed the 2007 Honest Leadership and Open Government Act requiring Senators and their staffs to take 'ongoing' ethics training. It included a long list of rule changes intended to rein-in corruption. Some Congress members don't fully understand what actions might constitute corruption and an annual training in ethics is warranted.[24]

New members of Congress receive a long talk before starting their duties on how the law works and their responsibilities and how to avoid the many temptations that are likely to spring up during their term in office.

Cases Illustrating Charges against Elected Officials

Tom DeLay, a former Texas congressman, served Texas' 22nd Congressional District from 1984 until 2006. He served as House majority leader from 2003 to 2005. He was nicknamed the Hammer and was known for deal-making and pork-barreling. In 2005, DeLay was charged with trying to influence Texas elections by funneling corporate money to various political candidates. In mid-August 2010, the Department of Justice ended a six-year investigation of

DeLay. Prosecutors held that the corporate money dispensed by DeLay helped the Republicans win control of the Texas House. The Republican majority then pushed through a congressional redistricting plan that sent more Republicans to Congress. The Department of Justice joined the lawsuits challenging the makeup of the map, claiming it unfairly draws minority communities out of certain districts. In 2006, Tom DeLay resigned from Congress after being indicted on money laundering and other charges involving campaign finance violations. He was sentenced to three years in prison, but remained free while awaiting appeal rulings. DeLay said that he raised and spent more than $12 million on legal fees since his first case with the House Ethics Committee in 1995. Yet in 2013, a Texas appellate court reversed his conviction and dropped the charges.

Senator Bob Menendez, a three-term U.S. Senator from New Jersey, Democratic, chaired the Senate's Foreign Relations Committee. He was put under investigation for intervening with federal officials to help a close friend, Florida ophthalmologist Salomon Melgen. Dr. Melgen, his family, and his company have donated hundreds of thousands of dollars to Senator Menendez and committees supporting him. Senator Menendez tried to help Melgen who was charged with padding his Medicare billing and over a Dominican port security contract. Senator Menendez took two personal trips to the Dominican Republic aboard Dr. Melgen's jet. He failed to disclose them as gifts. What this case illustrates is how beholden an elected official might be to defending the interests of heavy donors to their election campaign.[25]

CONCLUSION

Clearly, the American legislature is grossly ineffective in debating and passing legislation. Congress often goes on for years without addressing the serious long-term problems facing the American system, such as immigration, health reform, infrastructure deterioration, environmental protection, and others.

The following Congressional reforms would serve the American voters well:

- Prevent the sticking in of irrelevant measures to a major bill to force the other party to vote for something they don't want.
- Reduce filibustering and moves to shut down government.
- How about disclosing who is giving all the money? Let's have a bill that makes the source of all political money transparent so that we are not being influenced by foreign money, etc.

- Reverse *Citizens United* so that the amount of money going into elections is reduced.
- Congress hasn't yet acted to convert our system of measurement into the more universally used metric form.
- Congress is not facing up to the problem of 'inversions' where American companies are converting into foreign companies.
- Congress is not dealing with the trillions of dollars that American companies are not bringing back into the U.S. because of the high corporate tax. How about lowering the corporate tax rate so that the money can start coming back into the country?
- Congress cannot accomplish much in Washington, D.C. Members of Congress are in Washington Monday through Wednesday and return home for the rest of the week. It would be better to spend three weeks in Washington and three weeks back home.

NOTES

1   C. Hulse, 'Seeking to End Gerrymandering's Enduring Legacy', *New York Times*, January 26, 2016.
2   N. Madigan, 'Florida Court Finds Politics Determined District Lines', *New York Times*, July 9, 2015.
3   P. Krugman, 'Republicans Against Retirement', *New York Times*, August 17, 2015.
4   For more details, see M. Welsh, 'An Overview of the Development of U.S. Congressional Committees', *Law Library Lights*, 47, 3 & 4, Spring and Summer (2004). Law Librarians' Society of Washington, D.C. Inc. (www.llsdc.org/), July 2008.
5   A. Mitchell, 'With Ceremony, Clinton Signs Line-Item Veto Measure', *New York Times*, April 10, 1996.
6   M. Short and A. Koenig, 'Giving Billions to the Rich', *New York Times*, November 23, 2015.
7   See: http://en.wikipedia.org/wiki/United_States_federal_government_shutdown_of_2013 (accessed 03.03.16).
8   Editorial, 'A Shortage of Funds for Food Safety', *New York Times*, April 9, 2015.
9   R. Cox, 'GOP blocks Warren's student loan bill', *New York Times*, September 16, 2014.
10 Schumpeter, 'The Washington Wishing-Well: The Unstoppable Rise in Lobbying by American Business is Bad for Business Itself', *The Economist*, June 13, 2015.
11 Mark Mizruchi, *The Fracturing of the American Corporate Elite* (Harvard College, Cambridge, MA, 2013).

12   G. Easterbrook, 'Our Navy is Big Enough', *New York Times*, March 9, 2015. Also see: 'With $8.5 trillion unaccounted for, why should Congress increase the defense budget': www.thefiscaltimes.com/2015/03/19/85.

13   A good exposé book to read is C. Lewis, *The Buying of the Congress* (Avon Books, London, 1998). Also see J. Nichols and R. W. McChesney, *Dollarocracy: How the Money and Media Election Complex is Destroying America* (Nation Books, New York, 2013). Also see M. Salter, 'Sugar-Coated Capitalism is No Free Market', *Forbes*, November 16, 2015.

14   B. Allison and S. Harkins, 'Fixed Fortunes: Biggest Corporate Political Interests Spend Billions, get Trillions', *Sunlight Foundation*, November 17, 2014.

15   L. Drutman, *The Business of America is Lobbying* (Oxford University Press, Oxford, 2015).

16   F. Fukuyama, 'The Decay of the American Political Institutions', *The American Interest*, December 8, 2013.

17   R. D. Wolff, 'How the Rich Soaked the Rest of Us', *Guardian*, March 1, 2011. Also see Wolff's *Democracy at Work: A Cure for Capitalism* (Haymarket Books, Chicago, IL, 2012).

18   L. Lessig, *Republic Lost: How Money Corrupts Congress – and a Plan to Stop It* (Hachette, New York, 2011).

19   Z. Teachout, 'Legalized Bribery', *New York Times*, January 26, 2015.

20   See: http://en.wikipedia.org/wiki/lobbying#cite_note-twsNovZ111-22 (accessed 03.03.16).

21   See: http://en.wikipedia.org/wiki/lobbying#cite_note-23 (accessed 03.03.16).

22   Editorial, 'The I.R.S. Gives Up on "Dark Money"', *New York Times*, July 25, 2015.

23   S. Medvic, 'There is Very Little Corruption in U.S. Politics', *New York Times*, April 3, 2013. Medvic is the author of *In Defense of Politicians: The Expectations Trap and Its Threat to Democracy* (Routledge, New York, 2013).

24   D. N. Cicilline and S. Rigell, 'Teach Congress a Lesson', *New York Times*, January 2, 2015.

25   Editorial, 'Step Down, Senator Robert Menendez', *New York Times*, April 2, 2015.

CHAPTER 4

REFORMING THE EXECUTIVE BRANCH—IS THE PRESIDENT TOO POWERFUL?

'The measure of a man is what he does with power.'
Pittacus

As much as Congress is disliked, the sitting President also is often a target of unrestrained vituperation or disdain, especially the more effective he or she is in pressing for improved programs. America's greatest Presidents—Lincoln, Teddy Roosevelt, and Franklin Roosevelt—suffered from the scorn of large and wealthy groups. Today many critics heap scorn on Barack Obama. George Will, the conservative journalist, charges that President Obama uses 'executive authoritarianism to evade the Constitution's separation of powers and rewrite existing laws.'

Charles Krauthammer, another conservative journalist, claims that 'visionary thinkers like Obama cannot be bound by normal constitutional strictures.' The popular singer Ted Nugent called President Obama a 'subhuman mongrel.'[1]

In 2014, John Hawkins listed what was in his mind 50 examples of Obama corruption, dishonesty, and incompetence. Former NYC Mayor Rudy Giuliani created a storm with his statement: 'I know this is a horrible thing to say, but I do not believe that the President loves America...He wasn't brought up the way you were brought up and I was brought up through love of this country.' After Obama was elected, Mitch McConnell, the Senate Minority Leader, made this statement: 'our number one goal is to make Barack Obama a one-term President.'

The attacks on President Obama are extremely partisan. In spite of them, an increasing number of articles have appeared saying that Obama will go down as one of the strongest Presidents in our history. Several articles already list over 50 top accomplishments of his presidency.[2]

The disdainful attitude toward many of our Presidents highlights the long-term conflict that colors the relationship between Congress and the President. The majority party in Congress prefers a weak President who doesn't mess with the legislation they pass and who doesn't push for much new legislation. They see the President's job to be mainly executing the policies of the Congress. However, the fact is that a multitude of decisions have to be made in just executing Congress' policies.

To help in this task, a huge bureaucracy reports to the President. There are thousands of departments, offices, commissions, and committees entrusted with carrying out these policies. There are many regulations and the President has to decide how vigorously certain regulations should be budgeted for and implemented. Congress often prefers a relaxed application of regulations but some Presidents are intent in carrying out the spirit of the regulation.

THE POWERS AND RESPONSIBILITIES OF THE PRESIDENT UNDER THE CONSTITUTION

The U.S. President's powers and responsibilities are defined in Article II of the U.S. Constitution:

- Section 1 of Article II: Qualifications. Contains clauses covering the qualifications for office, salary determination, managing vacancy and disability questions, and taking an oath of office.
- Section 2 of Article II: Presidential Powers. Includes command of military, handling the opinions of cabinet secretaries, the power to grant pardons, the making of appointments, and the handling of treaties.
- Section 3 of Article II: President's Responsibilities. Includes reporting on the State of the Union, making recommendations to Congress, calling Congress into extraordinary session, adjourning Congress, receiving foreign representatives, and caring for the faithful execution of the law.
- Section 4 of Article II: Impeachment. Describes the conditions for impeachment.

Here we discuss each of the four sections of Article II.

SECTION 1 OF ARTICLE II: QUALIFICATIONS

The President of the U.S. must be born of parents who are U.S. citizens. The most controversial case arose with respect to whether Barack Obama was a natural-born citizen of the U.S. and was qualified to be President. Many conspiracy theories arose about whether his birth certificate was a forgery and whether he was actually born in Kenya or that he had become a citizen of Indonesia. Yet in April 2011 the Hawaii Department of Health released a certified copy of Obama's original Certificate of Live Birth and two Hawaii newspapers carried the birth announcement. In spite of this evidence, there still remain conspiracy theorists. A May 2011 Gallup poll found that 13% of American adults (23% of Republicans) continued to express doubts.

A more recent case centers on whether presidential candidate Ted Cruz is a 'natural born' citizen of the U.S. He was born in Canada. Only his mother is American. The case must still be decided.

Section 1 also discusses the President's salary determination. In recent times, the President of the U.S. drew a salary of $200,000 a year. This was raised to $400,000 when George W. Bush became President. In addition, the President receives a $50,000 non-taxable expense account. Upon retirement from office, former Presidents receive a pension, Secret Service protection, and reimbursements for staff, travel, mail, and office expenses. Their pension varies with the current salary of cabinet members, which was $191,300 annually as of March, 2008.

Many ex-Presidents continue to earn income by accepting speaking invitations. Bill Clinton would charge as much as $200,000 a speech. Another great source of income is publishing books: Bill and Hillary Clinton separately published bestselling books. We can imagine ex-Presidents earning more money by acting as lobbyists for a number of companies. Although presidential pay is low relative to CEO pay, it is made up later by an active presidential after-life. Jimmy Carter and Bill Clinton continued as concerned Americans using their ideas and personalities to back a variety of good causes around the world.

In the case of a presidential illness or disability, the statute is less clear. The framers felt that they solved the problem by providing for a Vice President to replace the President if necessary. Eight Presidents—Harrison, Taylor, Lincoln, Garfield, McKinley, Harding, Roosevelt, and Kennedy—died in office and were immediately replaced by the Vice President. This should emphasize the importance of Presidents choosing a very able Vice President as a running mate. Had John McCain won the presidency in 2008 against Barack Obama and died in office, Sarah Palin would have taken over, much to the consternation of most Americans.

The more interesting question is what should be done if the President seems to be losing his mental or physical capacity. President Garfield, shot by an assassin's bullet, was bedridden for 11 weeks, could do no work, and the government was without a leader. This also happened when President McKinley was shot at the beginning of his second term and died eight days later. President Kennedy later took these tragedies seriously and asked Congress to develop a clear procedure to handle these cases, resulting in the passage of the 25th Amendment.

The 25th Amendment concerns presidential disability, or what to do with the presidency if the President cannot perform his presidential duties. At one extreme, if the President was to contract Alzheimer's disease and not know what was going on, he would have to be replaced by the Vice President. But what if his mental or physical powers gradually grew less acute? Ronald Reagan was known to fall asleep at cabinet meetings and there was a hint of Alzheimer's disease which might have been hidden from the public.[3] Franklin D. Roosevelt was clearly losing his mental and physical energy in his fourth term as President. Given that many Presidents are elected at an older age, many in their seventies or eighties will slow down. This could lead citizens to favor younger candidates. Citizens showed a concern about potentially electing Bernie Sanders, who ran for President at the age of 74.

The 25th Amendment says that if the President feels unable to discharge the powers and duties of his office, he needs to send a written declaration to this effect to the President *pro tempore* of the Senate and the Speaker of the House of Representatives. At such time, the Vice President will be appointed as Acting President. But then if the President subsequently sends a written declaration to resume the powers and duties of his office, he will resume his position as President unless the Vice President and a majority of principal officers of the executive department decide that he should not resume the presidency and Congress proceeds to assemble and vote by a two-thirds majority in both chambers that the President is unable to discharge the powers and duties of his office. The Vice President will continue as the Acting President.

SECTION 2 OF ARTICLE II: PRESIDENTIAL POWERS

The Constitution clearly makes the President the Commander-in-Chief in military matters. The heads of the military branches all report to the President. But the President cannot declare war. Only Congress can declare war according to Article I, Section 8, Clause 11 of the U.S. Constitution. In 1973, The War Powers Act allows the President to use military forces for 60 days without a formal declaration of war by Congress. It also grants an additional 30 days upon a formal request by the President, regardless of Congress' agreement with the request. But it remains up to Congress to formally declare war. Yet the President can send troops. Back in 2002,

Congress passed the 'Congressional Authorization to Use Force in Iraq' resolution, which can be interpreted as a declaration of war, although it didn't use those explicit words. The U.S. has formally declared war against foreign nations five separate times, each upon a prior request by the President of the U.S.

The President also runs a cabinet of advisors consisting of department heads and others. The President appoints the department heads normally from his own party. Lincoln and Obama, among some other Presidents, did select certain department heads from the other party. The President is responsible for nominating the heads of governmental departments, which the Senate must then approve. The President nominates judges to federal courts and justices to the U.S. Supreme Court. The Constitution gives the President almost limitless power to give pardons for federal offenses without Congressional approval.

Both the Supreme Court and Congress watch carefully any efforts of the President to exceed his authority. In June 2014, the Court ruled that Obama exceeded his power in making three high-level appointments to the National Labor Relations Board (NLRB) during a Congressional recess. Congress did appear to take their regular recess, which does allow the President to make appointments, especially considering that he is often blocked on getting appointments through during regular Congressional sessions. Republicans held that a few Republican Congressmen were carrying on official business and therefore it was not true that Congress was in a full recess.

SECTION 3 OF ARTICLE II: PRESIDENT'S RESPONSIBILITIES

To carry on his work, the President can issue executive orders which have the force of law but do not have to be approved by congress. He is expected to deliver a State of the Union address annually to a joint session of Congress. He can convene special sessions of Congress. He can veto legislation approved by Congress. However, the veto is limited. It is not a line-item veto, meaning that he or she cannot veto only specific parts of legislation, and it can be overridden by a two-thirds vote by Congress.

The President also receives ambassadors and works with leaders of other nations. He has the power to make treaties with Senate approval. The U.S. currently takes part in 14 Free Trade Agreements (FTAs) with 20 countries. During 2015, President Obama was busy working on a major trade agreement with Asian countries called the Trans-Pacific Partnership (TPP). Senate members and others complained that Obama was proceeding without making the proposed treaty's terms sufficiently clear to them or to citizens. Obama obviously didn't want continuous debate on every provision while the treaty was being drafted. He preferred to delay the debate until the whole treaty proposal was ready for Senate debate and approval.

SECTION 3 OF ARTICLE II: IMPEACHMENT

Article II, Section 3 of the U.S. Constitution states that, 'The President, Vice President, and all civil Officers of the United States shall be removed from Office on Impeachment for, and Conviction of, Treason, Bribery, or other High Crimes and Misdemeanors.' The House of Representatives has the sole power of impeaching. A majority of the House must vote to impeach the President. The U.S. Senate has the sole power to try all impeachments and two-thirds must vote for conviction. The removal of impeached officials is automatic upon conviction in the Senate. If impeached, the President is never allowed to hold a government position again.

Andrew Johnson, our 17th President, was impeached while in office. He was found guilty by 35 senators, just one vote short of the two-thirds vote necessary to convict him. President Richard Nixon resigned from office rather than face impeachment charges in the Watergate scandal in 1974. President Bill Clinton became the second president to be impeached by the House in 1998. Later, the Senate found him not guilty.

HOW DOES CONGRESS TRY TO RESTRAIN THE PRESIDENT'S POWER?

The Constitution makes it clear that Congress has the exclusive power to make law and the job of the President is to execute the instructions of Congress. However, it is easy to see many situations where the legislation is loosely defined and the President has to fill in the details and exercise his or her opinion on Congressional intent.

Constitutional scholars believe that the Constitutional Convention of 1787 spent far more time and debate on the powers of Congress than on the powers of the President, perhaps because of the wish not to limit George Washington who was assumed to become the first President. The country was choosing a leader by popular vote, not by heredity or by force. This was something new. While Madison thought that the legislature would be dominant anyway, Alexander Hamilton preferred an executive with the power to match the monarchs of Europe.[4]

Over time power has flowed increasingly to the Executive Branch. The public has realized that Congress is no longer able to make timely responses in a rapidly changing insecure world. The President has to be free to respond quickly to new developments and threats. In addition, administering the laws requires a growing bureaucracy reporting to the President through the cabinet officers and others. Congress cannot oversee all the activities going on in conducting the nation's affairs. Finally, strong Presidents such as Lincoln and the two Roosevelts showed the reasonableness and necessity of presidential powers under different threats and circumstances.[5] The world is changing too quickly with new opportunities and new threats, requiring the President to be a proactive president, not just a President waiting for Congress to respond.

President Obama has undertaken policy initiatives to get around the gridlocked Congress. He announced a new policy to give undocumented parents of U.S. citizens permission to live and work for three years without fear of deportation if they met certain qualifications. Texas and 25 other states immediately sued, saying the President exceeded his authority. Instead of Congress using its voting power to stop the President from doing this, states have chosen to act as plaintiffs to ask courts to thwart the president's policies. Hopefully the Supreme Court will take up this issue and prevent court law suits against the President.

Two Cases of Congress–President Conflict

Youngstown Sheet & Tube Co. et al. v. Sawyer

In 1951–52, the steel workers' union was bargaining with the steel companies to seek better terms and conditions for workers. Efforts at resolution and mediation continued to fail. On April 4, 1952, the steelworkers gave notice of a nationwide strike to begin at 12.01 a.m., April 9, 1952. A few hours before the strike, President Harry Truman issued Executive Order 10340 directing the Secretary of Commerce to take possession and operate most of the nation's steel mills, claiming that it was necessary to avert a national catastrophe which would result from a stoppage of steel production. The fact that steel was a necessary component of all weapons led Truman to believe that the proposed work stoppage would immediately jeopardize our national defense. However, the mill owners objected and argued that the President's order amounted to lawmaking, a legislative function that was expressly confined to the Congress. The steel companies brought proceedings against the President in the District Court. The President said he was acting in his constitutional powers as the

(Continued)

(Continued)

nation's Chief Executive and the Commander in Chief of the Armed Forces. The next morning the President sent a message to Congress reporting his action. But Congress took no action.

The Supreme Court ruled that neither the Constitution nor the Congress granted power to the President to take possession and operate the assets of any company or industry. But was the seizure order within the constitutional power of the President regarding national security? The Court decided against allowing the President to do this and preferred to leave labor disputes to be settled by collective bargaining along with mediation, conciliation, investigation by boards of inquiry, public reports, and possibly temporary injunctions to provide cooling-off periods. When these tactics failed, unions were free to strike if their members voted to strike.[6]

New York Times v. United States

In 1971, President Nixon, wanted to prevent the *New York Times* and the *Washington Post* from publishing the contents of a classified study entitled 'History of U.S. Decision-Making Process on Vietnam Policy' on the grounds of the alleged harm it would do to national security. There is no question that the President has the responsibility of protecting national security. He has a right to resort to the Supreme Court to prohibit the publication of this material. Yet the Court wants to preserve the 1st Amendment guaranteeing freedom of speech. The Supreme Court would prefer that Congress passed a bill giving the President this power to restrain information bearing on national security.

But given no action by Congress, the Supreme Court has to decide, and it decided that the President had no right to prohibit the publication of the said document. In this case, the 1st Amendment on Freedom of Speech prevailed over the President's right to act to prevent what he thought would jeopardize national security.

IMPROVING THE RELATIONSHIP BETWEEN CONGRESS AND THE EXECUTIVE BRANCH

Congress is clearly very sensitive about any President taking actions or asserting powers that are not specifically defined by the Constitution or Congress that would have the effect of making new laws. Congress worries about a President who grows his power too much. This was Congress' view of the aggressive actions of Franklin Roosevelt during the Great Depression of the 1930s to propose many new laws and acts. Congress finally came down on him when Roosevelt proposed expanding the number of justices in the Supreme Court from 9 to 15 justices and to make other changes. The Supreme Court had struck down several New Deal pieces of legislation saying that the laws gave too much authority to the executive branch. Roosevelt won a landslide re-election in 1936 and proposed in February 1937 to retire at age 70 all justices over age 70 at full pay. Any justice refusing to retire would get an 'assistant' with full voting rights. Critics arose to charge Roosevelt with trying to 'pack the Court.' Roosevelt relented when two Supreme Court justices shifted to a liberal position in April 1936. In July, the Senate voted 70 to 22 against Roosevelt's court reorganization plan.

The President's personality has a lot to do with his ability to work with Congress. Democratic President Lyndon Johnson was very effective in cultivating many in Congress, including Republicans, to work with him on passing civil rights legislation. It is possible also that he knew a lot of secrets about specific Congressmen to assure that they would vote for his policies. On the other hand, Barack Obama faced many opponents during his terms of office. Republicans were miffed that their favorite candidate, John McCain, lost to this new Senator who had little experience in politics. They found Obama too anxious to push forward the ideas of the Democratic Party. They questioned even whether he was an American with such a strange name as Barack Obama. There was an undercurrent of prejudice about electing the first African-American president. Obama, on his side, seemed to operate with a few insiders and spend the rest of his time with his family. He didn't put in full time to meet and cultivate allies in Congress. He missed the Johnson touch.

Any new President immediately loses the support of the other party. Each party has its agenda and its mechanisms for securing a uniform vote for or against any bill. This problem has worsened into political gridlock in recent years, making it impossible for Congress to pass much-needed legislation. In earlier times, certain key Congressmen and women had gained respect from members of the other party. Think about how Senator Ted Kennedy was able to work with Congress members on the other side of the aisle. The basic norm is that both sides will have to compromise and they will be able to pass bills as long as each side can look good and even look like they were victorious.

HOW DOES THE PRESIDENT MANAGE EFFICIENCY IN THE BUREAUCRACY?

As the executive in charge of implementing federal policy, the President runs a huge bureaucracy consisting of thousands of departments, offices, commissions, committees, and other organizational units. Just within the government health system alone, there are over 16 offices to contact for further health information.[7] We are talking about a vast system of civil servants. All of the civil servants have passed tests regarding their qualifications and they all are well trained in their duties and responsibilities. Countries around the world differ in the quality level of their government employees with Singapore, Japan, Canada, Great Britain, and Scandinavian countries able to attract and retain good people who had good or better opportunities outside of government but who prefer to work as civil servants.[8]

The efficiency and effectiveness of government organizations depends not only on the way these organizations are structured and whether they have clear missions and goals, but also on the quality of public servants managing these organizations. Paul Light, in his book *A Government Ill-Executed*, writes that much stands in the way of attracting and keeping high-level people and staff in federal government organizations.

The first problem is that the nomination and confirmation process has become increasingly protracted, intrusive, acrimonious, and political. If a political party suspects that a nominee will be overly partisan to the President's policies, they will assail the candidate, threaten to filibuster, and protract the delay until the candidate or the President gives up. Many a highly-qualified candidate will either decline going after that appointment or will try and fail. Then the other party—usually Republicans—will say that government doesn't work well, when all along they have blocked the kinds of talented individuals who could really run a department with efficiency and effectiveness.

The second problem is that the government pay scale may also involve the candidate taking a pay cut. A highly-qualified Professor at a major university might have to accept a 20–50% pay cut to accept a government appointment. He or she can earn much more in private industry.

The third problem is the rule-based nature of many government departments that can limit the power of an effective new administrator to make the changes that he or she wants to make. Out of frustration with government bureaucracy, the new department head will opt for a short tenure and leave government sooner than planned. And the President may be powerless to help this person stay longer and give the challenge more effort.[9]

CONCLUSION

Congress is often hard on a new President because either their candidate lost or Congress wants to make it clear early on that it is to be the only or major source of new laws. Because many new laws are not well defined, the President will have to execute them and interpret their intent. Congress may not like the President's interpretation or not agree with which programs the President spends most of his time executing. Furthermore, new events and situations often require the President to take early or immediate action because Congress is normally much slower to move or act. So there are many reasons why tension exists between the President and Congress. A new President has the choice of showing full respect to Congress and therefore getting little done, or pushing hard to get Congressional action and draw their enmity. A large factor lies in how well the American public likes its President. A smart President will carefully cultivate members of his party and the other party and make decisions that ultimately will win the public's support.

NOTES

1   Morgan Whitaker, 'Ted Nugent calls Obama "subhuman mongrel"', MSNBC, January 22, 2014.
2   See: Paul Glastris, Ryan Cooper, and Siyu Hu, 'Obama's Top 50 Accomplishments', *Washington Montly*, March April, 2012.
3   K. Moisse, 'Could Someone Run the Country with Alzheimer's Disease?', *ABC News Medical Unit*, January 17, 2011. Reagan was diagnosed with Alzheimer's six years after finishing his second term. His son, Ron Reagan, said that he saw early signs of Alzheimer's while his father was still in office.
4   'Exploring Constitutional Conflicts': http://law2.umkc.edu/faculty/projects/ftrials/conlaw/prespowers.html (accessed 03.03.16).
5   Ibid.
6   See the Youngstown case: http://law2.umkc.edu/faculty/projects/ftrials/conlaw/youngstown.html (accessed 03.03.16).
7   See: www.data.gov.
8   Editorial, 'Civil-service Reform: Modernizing the Mandarins', *The Economist*, August 9, 2014, p. 51.
9   See H. Pollack, 'Why it's Rare for Someone Like Ashton Carter to Work in Government', *Washington Post*, December 5, 2014.

CHAPTER 5

REFORMING THE FEDERAL JUDICIARY PROCESS—IS THE JUDICIARY SHAPING LEGISLATION?

'Do not judge, and you will never be mistaken.'
Jean Jacques Rousseau

The Courts represent the third branch of government and they function to provide a check-and-balance system to the Congress and the presidency. The Courts can be asked to decide whether a particular law passed by Congress is compatible with the Constitution, whether a particular presidential action is compatible with the Constitution, and whether a particular State's action is compatible with the Constitution. When the Supreme Court rules that something passed by Congress is unconstitutional, it looks like the Supreme Court is actually creating or shaping legislation, a function that technically belongs to Congress. The Supreme Court has also overruled presidential action from time to time as unconstitutional.

When the President appointed three members of the National Labor Relations Board during a recess of the Senate, Congress said that it still had a few Congress legislators carrying on Congressional work and therefore the President overstepped. The Supreme Court ruled that President Obama overstepped in making his three appointments because Congress was 'in session.'

Article 3 of the Constitution provides that, 'the judicial power of the United States, shall be vested in one Supreme Court, and in such inferior Courts as the Congress may from time to time ordain and establish.' The 'inferior Courts' include federal district, bankruptcy, and circuit courts that first hear about 1.3 million cases a year. The Court receives an average of 7,000 to 8,000 petitions in each term, but fewer than 80 are set for full briefing and oral argument. To be selected as a case, at least four of the justices must agree on hearing that case.

Today the Supreme Court consists of nine justices nominated by the President and confirmed by the Senate. The U.S. Constitution says nothing about the Supreme Court having nine justices. The number has varied over time, including a time when President Franklin Roosevelt tried to add another six members to the Court but it was defeated by a Democratic controlled Congress. The Court is the final arbiter of the law and is charged with ensuring the American people the promise of equal justice under the law. The Constitution does not say that the Court is the final arbiter but this tradition was established by Chief Justice John Marshall who ran the early Supreme Court for 35 years (he was the fourth Chief Justice). The Supreme Court's power was confirmed in 1803 when Marshall's Court voted unanimously in *Marbury v. Madison*. Marshall's Court ruled that the Court could declare acts of Congress unconstitutional even though the Constitution does not give the Supreme Court the power to do so.

One can question whether the nine justices are broadly experienced enough to represent the vast range of U.S. opinion. Virtually all the current justices went to Harvard or Yale. Most of them are from New York. Almost all of them were justices before the appointment. In the past, virtually all the justices were Protestant. Today six of the current justices are Catholic, and three are Jewish, raising the question of where Protestants and other religious groups, including atheists, are represented. In the past, all the justices were men; today three of the justices are women. All this raises questions about whether the nine justices have a sufficient range of work and life experiences to fairly represent the varied interests of our nation. Or put another way, shouldn't there be more diversity in the Court?

The Court becomes active in early October and renders decisions in the argued cases by the end of June. The Court must continuously balance society's need for security and order with the individual's right to freedom. The Court has the power of 'judicial review' but must also try to maintain a 'living Constitution' that fits and addresses new problems that the framers of the Constitution might never have expected. Therefore, the Court is involved in constitutional interpretation. The Court has the jurisdiction to declare cases and controversies involving constitutional issues. The Court does not give advisory opinions but rather decisions in specific cases. It alone must decide in cases involving disputes between states or between a state and the federal government.

Most people see the Supreme Court as having made good decisions. The Court struck down whites-only party primaries and insisted that black and white children are to be educated in the same classrooms. It legalized same-sex marriage and in many cases supported fair voting. Yet there was an earlier time when the Court upheld poll taxes and literacy tests. The most trenchant criticism is that the Court's majority largely favors the interest of big business and corporations. Witness the *Citizens United* 5-to-4 decision where corporations, unions, and associations can spend huge amounts to influence elections. The Court's rulings have not always been exemplary. Fortunately, 60% of the Fortune 300 companies agreed not to donate company money.

ARE THE JUSTICES STRICTLY INDEPENDENT OR LARGELY PARTISAN?

Justices take one of two views in interpreting and applying the Constitution to individual cases. Justices are called 'originalists' or 'textualists' when they go back to the literal words in the Constitution and try to determine the intended fixed meaning as of the time when the Constitution was adopted. They want to arrive at an interpretation that is consistent with what the framers meant when they drafted and ratified the Constitution. They might include interpreting what reasonable persons living at the time would have taken the text to mean. Originalism is popular among many political conservatives in the U.S., and is associated mostly with justices Clarence Thomas and the late Antonin Scalia.

The non-originalists argue that a Constitution should be a more living document that adapts to new conditions and issues that were not present over 200 years ago. For the Constitution to endure over time, interpretations must be more flexible and responsive to changing circumstances. How could we know what the framers would have thought about whether men and women doing the same work should receive equal pay or about whether same-sex marriage is an acceptable interpretation of the meaning of marriage? The 14th Amendment of the Constitution passed in 1868 further opened citizen rights with the statement that no state 'can deprive any person of life, liberty or property, without due process of law.' But even this amendment is subject to many judicial interpretations of citizen's rights. Non-originalists on the Supreme Court tend to be more flexible in their interpretation of the original Constitution and its amendments.

Returning to the question of whether justices are free of political ideologies in their decision making, the answer is no. The justices tend to be partisan in their views; just observe the number of times that the Court vote is 5 to 4 by roughly the same justices. The five justices who were appointed by more conservative presidents tend to vote as a group even though they may have different reasons to reach the same conclusion. The same hold true for the four justices who received their appointments from more liberal Presidents. One study found that judges tend to be more conservative than lawyers, which means that a conservative bias prevails in our courts.[1]

How to remedy this partisan thinking is to appoint future justices who have a record of being more open minded in their decision making. Justice Anthony Kennedy is a good example of a justice who will sometimes vote with one group and at other times with the other group. He has generally supported the conservative majorities, but he has occasionally sided with the Court's more liberal members on such issues as same-sex marriage and a few other issues.

The fact is that there is no way to eliminate subjectivity in the judging process. Nine court members all read the same documents about a case and come to different opinions because of their different experiences and views. Concepts such as 'cruel and unusual punishment' or 'unreasonable searches and seizures' are subject to changing opinion over time. Every court case raises a myriad of considerations and the Court is often deciding whether the benefits to society of intervening are more important than protecting the right to privacy. It is wrong to think that justices just apply the law; they also make the law. The values and views of the judges matter enormously. There is no such thing as objective judging.[2]

The Supreme Court, just like the President, has often been accused of overstepping its power. Senator Ted Cruz of Texas denounced the Court as 'lawless' and 'brazen' in 2015 after hearing of the Court's rulings on the Affordable Care Act and same-sex marriage. Cruz argued that threatened 'the very foundations of our representative form of government.' He issued a call for a constitutional amendment that would remove the justices' life tenure and subject them to retention elections. The idea of a retention vote for justices is awful because justices would then be influenced in their decisions by their wish to be re-elected. The whole purpose of the life tenure is to insulate the justices from political pressure and keep them independent.

A less radical step would be to put a term limit on how long a supreme justice can remain on the bench. One possibility is to retain individual justices up to the age of say 80. Since most justices receive their appointment when they are around 50, they would have a 30-year career on the Supreme Court. Another proposal called for limiting them to a term of 18 years. This means they will be rendering judgments during the terms of three to five presidents.

THE ROLE OF THE SUPREME COURT IN ADVANCING CAUSES

There are many public issues that the Supreme Court does not put on its calendar, such as the status of illegal parent and children immigrants. The Court doesn't act and Congress prefers to kick the can down the road. The President is also stymied because all he can do is try to pressure Congress into action, and this usually doesn't work.

Political polls very often show that the public substantially favor a new set of rights. The solution finally arrives in the form of an important case which the Supreme Court decides on. If Congress lacks the courage and will to deal with major issues, the Court is the safety net to protect the rights of the people. When the Supreme Court recognized the right to marry for same-sex couples, this became constitutional and Congress had to accept it, in spite of some members of Congress crying foul and wanting to punish the Court for its independence. The point is that if a strong majority of Americans publicly favor a position and Congress is too lax or tied up to act, the Supreme Court comes in often as the major initiator of change.[3]

Those who think that the Supreme Court has too much power have proposed possible amendments to curb this power, including: allowing a two-thirds majority of the states to override a Supreme Court decision; prohibiting Congress from regulating activity that occurs wholly within one state; and requiring a seven-justice supermajority for Supreme Court decisions that invalidate a democratically enacted law. So far, none of these have passed.[4]

Three Supreme Court Cases

The *Roe v. Wade* case (1973)

Most states have rules limiting abortion in various ways. The Supreme Court in 1973 accepted a case involving a Texas law banning abortion except in the case of rape or incest. The Supreme Court, in a 7-to-2 decision, ruled that the Texas law restricting abortion violated the 14th Amendment of the U.S. Constitution. Section 1 of the 14th Amendment reads:

> All persons born or naturalized in the United States, and subject to the jurisdiction thereof, are citizens of the United States and of the state wherein they reside. No state shall make or enforce any law which shall abridge the privileges or immunities of citizens of the United States; nor shall any state deprive any person of life, liberty, or property, without due process of law; nor deny to any person within its jurisdiction the equal protection of the laws.

Thus no state can abridge the privileges of citizens or deprive them of life, liberty, or property without due process of law. A woman would have 'the liberty' of deciding

(Continued)

(Continued)

how to use 'her property' (i.e. her body). She could choose to have an abortion if she wanted it. She would not have to bear an unwanted child or resort to an illegal abortion with all of its risks. The justices, however, recognized the state's legitimate interest in protecting prenatal life and protecting a woman's health. Knowing that an abortion done later in pregnancy might injure a woman's health or hurt a viable fetus, the Court decided that a state could bar abortions after 24 or 28 weeks.

The Supreme Court's decision was hailed as a victory by 'pro-choice' citizens. Many family planning clinics were established to give advice and to perform careful abortions. Yet a large 'pro-life' citizen group grew to protest these 'abortion clinics' and gathered to give menacing glances at women entering these clinics, and in a few cases doctors who performed these operations were threatened and one was murdered. Legislators in states favoring the 'right to life' keep trying to add more restrictions to abortions, some even saying that a rape or incest provided no grounds for permitting an abortion. Several states require women seeking an abortion to make two visits to a clinic before she can have an abortion. In Texas, she would have to view her own fetus by submitting to an ultrasound 24 hours before deciding to have an abortion. Furthermore, the doctor must read state-mandated information about the medical risks of an abortion and alternatives to abortion, including offering the baby for adoption. Other states require the clinic to have state-of-the-art medical equipment to ensure that the woman's health is well protected during the surgery. This Texas provision recently led to the closing of several Texas clinics that could not afford to meet the stringent equipment standards of hospitals. The Supreme Court in 2016 will review the constitutionality of the Texas provision.

Pro-lifers argue that a person's life begins at conception, namely as a fertilized egg. They say there is 'personhood' and the state cannot 'deprive' that born person of 'life, liberty, or property.' If one agrees that the person is born at conception, there is a valid conflict about whose rights are paramount, the woman or the fetus. If the woman prevails, she would go on living but the other person, her fetus, will die. Note that the idea of personhood taking place at conception is a religious concept, not a scientific idea in that the fertilized egg has no personality or character, only potential. All nine justices ruled that a fetus is not a person. The late Justice Scalia argued that by a person, the framers of the 14th Amendment meant a 'walk-around' person, and by no intention meant a fertilized egg.

The Supreme Court has not ruled recently on subsequent restrictions passed by states, although they are under review by lower courts. This case shows how the Supreme Court comes into disputes with state rights people who would prefer that the people in every state should have the right to determine how they want to handle abortions. Those women in a state that has severely limited abortion rights can choose to have the surgery in an 'abortion rights' state. This is what a middle class woman is likely to do. But this ignores the large number of poor pregnant women who want to terminate their pregnancy but lack the finances to travel for the surgery in another state. This issue is likely to be unresolved for a long time. On the one hand you have the pro-choice people who would want a national law that abortion is legal with no conditions, versus on the other hand the pro-lifers who would want a national law that abortion is per se illegal wherever it takes place.

Supreme Court recognizes the right of same-sex marriage

On Friday June 26, 2015, the Supreme Court in a 5-to-4 vote recognized the nationwide right to same-sex marriage. Same-sex couples could marry in 16 states, but other states did not allow this or give recognition to same-sex marriages performed elsewhere. This decision made same-sex marriage a reality in the 34 states which had banned it. Justice Anthony M. Kennedy, who wrote for the majority, gave the most eloquent expression for this decision: 'No union is more profound than marriage, for it embodies the highest ideals of love, fidelity, devotion, sacrifice, and family. In forming a marital union, two people become something greater than once they were.' He went on to say that marriage is a 'keystone of our social order' and the plaintiffs were seeking 'equal dignity in the eyes of the law.' Justice Kennedy authored three of the Supreme Court's previous gay rights landmark decisions, including striking down one law in Texas that made gay sex a crime.

Public opinion had been changing rapidly and 21 other countries have recognized the right of same-sex marriage. Polls in the U.S. indicated that most Americans approved of same-sex marriage. But the four justices who voted against this decision displayed emotions ranging from dismay to scorn. Chief Justice John G. Roberts Jr. said that those in favor can celebrate but that the Constitution has nothing to do with this issue. He saw the decision as an act of will, not legal judgment. He said that people of faith can take no comfort with this decision, as if it might hurt religious liberty. He believed that gay rights activists would have achieved a more convincing victory through using the political process state by state.

The late Justice Antonin Scalia mocked Justice Kennedy's soaring language as pretentious and egotistic. Joined by Justice Clarence Thomas, Justice Scalia wrote that the Court's majority had discovered 'a "fundamental right" overlooked by every person alive at the time of ratification, and almost everyone else in the time since.' Scalia was defending the 'originalist' view of the Court, whereas Kennedy embraced a vision of 'a living Constitution.' Kennedy was saying that the Bill of Rights and the 14th Amendment implies an

(Continued)

(Continued)

expanding view of the right of all persons to enjoy and exercise liberty. He also argued that it was important that children adopted by same-sex couples know that their parents are married and not suffer from the stigma of having lesser status.

Republican presidential candidates for the 2016 election howled at the decision. Former Arkansas Governor Mike Huckabee demanded that people 'resist and reject judicial tyranny.' Wisconsin Governor Scott Walker uttered, 'The only alternative left for the American people is to support an amendment to the U.S. Constitution to reaffirm the ability of the states to continue to define marriage.'

This case clearly shows how Supreme Court decisions make new law, which technically is the prerogative of Congress. According to Kennedy, same-sex marriage is guaranteed by the Constitution. According to Roberts, the Constitution has nothing to say about same-sex marriage.

Supreme Court decision on the Affordable Care Act (ACA)

The Patient Protection and Affordable Care Act was passed by Congress and signed into law by President Obama on March 23, 2010. The new law aimed to meet the problem that over 40 million Americans carried no health insurance and were either neglecting their health or going to hospitals for emergency care. The new law also aimed to stop private health insurance companies from denying insurance to many people with pre-existing conditions.

The law set up a system where every citizen could get health insurance coverage on their own selected terms. Those who could not afford health insurance would be subsidized while others would be required to buy health insurance or pay a penalty.

To help offset the costs of unhealthy individuals, the law had to require most people to buy insurance or pay an annual penalty for not having coverage. The law provides subsidies to low- and middle-income families, and these subsidies are paid directly to insurers who then apply the discount to their customers' monthly premiums. On average, the subsidies reduced the price of monthly premiums by nearly 75%.

The government set up an online process for joining ACA and, after some computer glitches, made it easier to join. The government's plan was to work with each state setting up an exchange that would handle citizen payments and subsidies. Many states accepted this arrangement while other states refused to work with the government. They didn't want the federal government to dictate how their state would serve the medical needs of their citizens.

The Affordable Care Act aimed to create marketplaces, or exchanges, where people could shop for individual and family health insurance if they didn't have another source of coverage. The law wanted the states to set up their own exchanges. The federal government would set up exchanges in states that didn't build their own. The exchanges would provide subsidies to citizens who lacked the means to buy their own health insurance coverage. The ACA said that the subsidies would only be issued in states that set up exchanges.

Ever since the ACA was passed in 2010, Republicans in Congress attempted to repeal or weaken it. They refused to treat health care as a right. Yet the American people voted in 2008 to elect a President who promised to create a national right to health insurance coverage, and voted in 2012 to re-elect him over a candidate who promised to undo it. In spite of this, the Republicans brought three cases to the Supreme Court in order to demolish it. In 2012, the case challenged the individual mandate requiring everyone to buy health insurance and the Court rejected the challenge.

In the most recent case, *King v. Burwell*, four Virginians were the plaintiffs who did not want to buy health insurance. They argued that they were not eligible to receive a subsidy in their state, which had not set up an exchange, and therefore they did not have to buy health insurance.

On June 25, 2015, the justices rejected this challenge by a vote of 6 to 3. They made it clear that subsidies would be available in all states. The Obama administration said that a reading of the entire law makes it clear that subsidies are available in all exchanges, regardless of who's running them. The law was intended to extend health insurance to as many Americans as possible. Approximately 8 million people across America would lose their health insurance had the Court held in favor of the plaintiffs. The insurance market would have been wrecked. Lower-income and healthier enrollees would quickly drop their coverage. Insurers in turn would have to raise their rates to cover the costs, pricing even more people out of coverage and causing problems for the individual insurance market outside of just the exchanges.

Chief Justice John Roberts along with Justice Kennedy surprised everyone in agreeing with the Obama administration. He said that Congress would not have set up a system of insurance that would only function in states that had set up exchanges. He wrote, 'Congress passed the Affordable Care Act to improve health insurance markets, not to destroy them.'[5]

Although many conservatives were mad, many conservative strategists and politicians are quietly relieved. They would have been exposed for not having a plan to replace the subsidies that millions of Americans would have lost. Clearly, the Court has shown a willingness to support Congress in its 2010 decision to pass the Affordable Care Act and to make it work.

CONCLUSION

The Supreme Court rulings in 2015 hint at a change in the attitude of some Supreme Court justices toward how to view the Constitution. The U.S. Constitution was developed at a time when Americans had slaves, women couldn't vote, and American Indians had no rights. Since that time, so many new institutions, technologies, and mindsets have developed that the framers of the Constitution could not have foreseen. When the Constitution was formed, there were no automobiles, radio, television, movies, airplanes, computers, or the Internet. It is impossible to know what the framers would have decided in the millions of cases that have come up bearing on these new entities and ideas.

This has led to two different views on how to interpret the Constitution. The originalists choose to cling to the words and the intent of the founders in interpreting the Constitution. They have been criticized as treating the Constitution as a 'straightjacket.' The non-originalists prefer to treat the Constitution as a 'living document' that opens up to new and expanded views about life and values. Over time our views of liberty and equality keep expanding. Many Americans now hold that two persons of the same sex can marry, and this expands our view of liberty. Many now recognize that a working woman should have the same pay as a working man in the same job, and this expands our view of equality. We see the rights of liberty and equality as conferring dignity to all people, a belief in their self-value.

Another issue is how much judicial intervention the Courts should engage in. Congress would prefer that the Supreme Court minimize their judicial intervention. Congress typically passes laws that represent the will of the people and if Congress is wrong, Congressional members will suffer at election time. The President is more likely to favor judicial intervention when the Congress prevents the President from undertaking an action that would be in the interest of all or the vast majority of people. In the end, the hope is that the Supreme Court will continue to choose cases whose resolution is important if not urgent, so that fundamental issues are finally resolved.

Another issue is whether the justices should be appointed for life. The original thinking was that justices would be more independent with a lifetime appointment than they would be if they had to run for re-election. People today live longer and are able to work for a longer part of their life. On the other hand, mental and physical faculties tend to diminish with age. A justice's mental acuity can diminish or the justice could experience senility or Alzheimer's disease. Or a justice can experience physical ailments or impairments that interfere with having the time and energy to give full consideration to court issues. One could hope that a justice or the justice's family knows when a justice should retire from the Supreme Court. A number of suggestions have been made. Perhaps all justices should retire at age 80 or after being on the Court for a term of (say) 18 years. This would require a Constitutional amendment and it is not likely to happen in the near future, if ever.

The question remains: Is it better to let nine justices decide on what is right for the American people than rely on what a highly diversified group of 435 Representatives and 100 Senators have determined? My opinion is that the Court provides the country with the opportunity to deeply explore a major issue and make a decision. The Court's job is to decide on the Constitutionality of the issue. If the decision does not sit well with the public, they cannot do much about it without passing an amendment to the Constitution. Our Constitution's prime purpose is to reflect majority opinion subject to protecting minority rights.

NOTES

1 A. Liptak, 'Why Judges Tilt to the Right', *New York Times*, February 1, 2015, p. 6.
2 See E. Chemerinsky, 'There is No Such Thing as Objective Judging', *Constitutional Daily*, November 18, 2014.
3 The Supreme Court, 'Change is Gonna Come', *The Economist*, July 4, 2015.
4 C. Rampell, 'Tea Partyers Want a More Perfect Constitution', *My San Antonio*, January 18, 2016.
5 For an excellent analysis of the Roberts Court, see L. Tribe and J. Matz, *Uncertain Justice: The Roberts Court and the Constitution* (Picador, New York, 2014).

CHAPTER 6

REFORMING THE FEDERAL–STATES RELATIONSHIP—ARE THE STATES TOO INDEPENDENT?

'Only in the frictionless vacuum of a nonexistent abstract world can movement or change occur without that abrasive friction of conflict.'
Saul Alinsky

One of the reasons that the Articles of Confederation of May 1787 failed is that it gave too much power to the states. A stronger federal government was needed and it called for a new Constitution. The framers of the Constitution fought passionately over the balance of power between the states and the federal government. The 10th Amendment provided that powers not given to the federal government remain with the states or the people. This is still the understanding but many issues arise about whether Congress can require U.S. states to do something that states feel is their right to decide. For example, the law says that women have a right to abortion but each state has been free to establish different rules concerning conditions for abortion. Today Congress recognized the freedom of same-sex couples to marry but different states may resist or choose to be lax in its implementation.

Yet many U.S. states—among them Oklahoma, Texas, Montana, Utah—are unhappy about the size and power of the federal government. Some people have even advocated that the Southern states once again consider seceding from the U.S. They see the federal government as too big, too inefficient and too regulatory. They say that bureaucrats from Washington run too much of our economy. There is a feeling that governors and mayors run their states and cities more efficiently and are in closer touch with the needs of their people. There is a growing preference for more regional and local control. This means transferring more power from the federal government to state and local governments.

Much like the framers of the Constitution, America continues to debate the proper balance between federal and state powers. The basic understanding is that the Constitution makes it clear that the federal government can only pass laws of certain kinds and everything else is left to the states.

HOW CAN A NEW AMENDMENT TO THE CONSTITUTION BE PASSED?

The Constitution carefully defines how a new amendment can be passed and become the law of the land. Here are the two procedures:

- The Congress can propose amendments to the Constitution whenever two-thirds of both Houses shall deem it necessary.
- Or when two-thirds of the legislatures of the states shall call a convention for proposing amendments.

In either case, the amendment shall be valid when ratified by the legislatures of three-quarters of the states or by conventions in three-quarters of the states.

Note that unlike the passage of laws and regulations that can be passed or amended by a simple majority in Congress, the Constitution is difficult to change. The evidence of this conservative tendency is found by the fact that the Constitution only contains 27 Amendments in its 225-year history. The first ten Amendments constituted the Bill of Rights and were passed by Congress on September 25, 1789, and ratified on December 15, 1791. The remaining Amendments, 11–27, were passed by Congress during different administrations. The last Amendment, number 27, passed in 1992, dealt with Congressional pay raises and stated that the compensation of Senators and Representatives cannot be varied until an election of Representatives 'shall have intervened.' In other words, Congress cannot raise (or lower) its compensation until another election has taken place.

All this makes it clear that most proposed reforms are not likely to take place through passing a new amendment. Most reformers will have to search for more down-to-earth reform actions.

STATES DIFFER IN WHAT THEY WANT

States are pretty much left free to determine what they and their citizens want. This makes sense because states differ greatly in their political and cultural histories and economic resources and incomes. Americans treasure their freedoms and don't want to see the federal government impose uniform conditions on all states regarding each issue. Justice Louis D. Brandeis called states 'laboratories of democracy.' They provide testing grounds for innovations that other states can try and even the federal government can consider.[1]

In this spirit, the House of Representatives is considering a plan to cut back federal regulation of education and give state and local authorities more discretion over assessing teachers' and student, performance. John Kline, Republican of Minnesota and Chairman of the House Education Committee, said that this plan would 'provide American families the education system they deserve, not the one Washington wants.'[2]

At the same time, the great variation in U.S. state solutions to major problems comes at a cost. Here are some examples:

• Same-sex marriages are legal in some U.S. states but not in others. What happens to a same-sex married couple who moves to a state that doesn't recognize their marriage? What might make most sense is to require the new state to treat all married couples coming in from another state as legally married.

• Abortion laws vary widely from state to state in the U.S. A woman living in Indiana cannot get her abortion costs covered unless her life is endangered, she is raped, or has committed incest, but she can go to Illinois for her abortion and be fully funded. Different states put different requirements as to how late an abortion can be done, whether her parents have to approve of it, whether the woman must go through a waiting period, and so on.

• Each state defines what it considers to be a core curriculum for its students. Some states put a high emphasis on STEM courses (Science, Technology, Engineering, and Mathematics) while others just work on the basics of reading, writing, and arithmetic. The federal government wants to define a standard core curriculum for all states describing what K-12 students should know at the end of each grade in the English language, arts and mathematics (later they will define this for social studies and science). The idea is to ensure that students graduating from high school are prepared for college or to enter the workforce. Even though the move to a Common Core State Standards initiative is supported by the National Governors Association (NGA) and the Council of Chief State School Officers (CCSSO), there is much opposition in different states to this initiative. Some conservatives see this as a federal 'top-down' takeover of state and local education systems. South Carolina Governor Nikki Haley said her state should not 'relinquish control of education to the federal government, neither should we cede it to the consensus of other states.' Meanwhile, the Thomas B. Fordham Institute sees the Common Core Standards 'as clearly superior to those currently in use […] in both math and reading.'[3]

• A major problem today is whether marijuana can be grown and used for medical or recreational purposes. A number of states—Colorado, Washington State, Alaska, and Oregon—voted in favor of making recreational use of marijuana legal. Yet Congress and the Obama administration are too timid to push for a federal law on this topic. Technically, the Department of Justice can prosecute businesses and individuals handling marijuana of committing a federal crime. Needed is a bill to allow states to legalize marijuana for medical and recreational use. Or Congress can approve a provision to prevent the Department of Justice from preventing states from developing their own policies. Ultimately, marijuana should be removed from the Controlled Substances Act where it is classified as a drug like heroin and LSD. This would make it easier for U.S. states to decide how they want to regulate it.[4]

- Each U.S. state and city defines its own gun laws. The right to keep and bear arms is protected by the 2nd Amendment to the U.S. Constitution. Yet there are a number of federal statutes regulating the manufacture, trade, possession, transfer, record keeping, transport, and destruction of firearms, ammunition, and firearms accessories. They are enforced by the Bureau of Alcohol, Tobacco, Firearms and Explosives (ATF). In 1994, the government passed the Federal Assault Weapons Ban that banned semiautomatic assault weapons and large capacity ammunition feeding devices. However, the law expired in 2004, leaving states and cities freer to define their own gun laws.

CONCLUSION

We can see that U.S. states have a great deal of freedom to define their own laws regarding such issues as alcohol and hard drugs, evolution and creationism, freedom of speech and hate speech, permits for marches and rallies, public dress, campaign finance, prayer in the public schools, financial aid to religious schools, and many others. This puts a burden on those individuals and families moving to another state to recognize that the laws in the new state may differ quite significantly from those in their previous state. This also puts a major burden on millions of businesses doing interstate commerce to recognize the differing requirements for operating their business in the different states. It is not likely that states will give up their right to establish laws and statutes that meet their citizens' preferences rather than buy into federal efforts to increase uniformity. This issue will not go away as long as there is a U.S. federal government and separate state governments.

What is equally interesting is that a U.S. state legislature often wants to pass a uniform state law with which many of its cities disagree. A state may want to ban smoking but several of its cities might object. Or a state might want to permit the easy sale of guns but some of its cities may want to ban the sale of guns.

States often try to pre-empt the power of local governments to avoid conforming. A state like Texas might want to be a friendly state to attract business but many Texas cities might want to pass heavy anti-pollution laws. So just as the federal government might want states to conform to certain standards, state governments face the same problem in getting their cities to conform.[5]

NOTES

1   A. Chatterji, 'Don't Look to States for New Ideas', *The New York States*, January 12, 2015.

2   T. Lewin, 'More Conflict Over Cutting Federal Role in Education', *New York Times*, February 24, 2015.

3   S. Banchero, 'School-standards Pushback', *The Wall Street Journal*, March 23, 2013; M. Malkin, 'Lessons from Texas and the Revolt Against Common Core Power Grab', *Noozhawk*, March 24, 2013; T. B. Fordham Institute, 'State of State Standards & the Common Core in 2010—Executive Summary', August 26, 2013.

4   Editorial, 'Congress and Obama Are Too Timid on Marijuana Reform', *New York Times*, August 8, 2015.

5   S. Dewan, 'States are Overturning Local Law, Often at Behest of Industry', *New York Times*, February 24, 2015.

CHAPTER 7

REFORMING POLITICAL PARTIES—ARE THE PARTIES TOO RIGID?

'The two real political parties in America are the Winners and the Losers.'
Kurt Vonnegut

I t is well known that the framers of the Constitution did not like political parties. There is nothing said about parties in the Constitution. Yet most countries today have two or more political parties. China and Russia are exceptions.

As individuals, citizens have very little ability to influence public policy. But they will recognize other citizens in the population who espouse similar views to theirs. They are likely to join them in initially representing an interest group. It might be an interest group that wants to reduce pollution and environmental harm. This group might seek some political influence in government delibera-tions. They may establish themselves as a Green Party and seek more members and recruits. Another interest group may be bent on preserving individual freedom and may attract others and grow into a Libertarian Party.

It's important to recognize that most countries have multiple parties, not just two. Consider Italy as an example. Italian politics between 1945 and 1994 was dominated by two major parties: Christian Democracy, which was the party of government; and the Italian Communist Party, which was the main opposition party. There was another opposition party, the post-fascist Italian Social Movement. The Christian Democracy party chose its coalition partners from among four parties: the Italian Socialist Party, the Italian Democratic Socialist Party, the Italian Republican Party, and the Italian Liberal Party. Today the pic-ture is more complex. Eight major parties exist (defined as those having gathered more than 4% in the last general election): Democratic Party, Five Star Movement, Forward Italy, Northern League, New Centre-Right, Civic Choice, Left Ecology Freedom, and Brothers of Italy. In addition, there are 33 minor parties, with such names as Pensioners' Party, Party of Italian Communists, New Italian Socialist Party, and Green Italy.[1]

In such a multi-party system, no single party can win a majority. Instead each major party has to form coalitions with other parties that are not too different. The coalition must agree on the coalition leader and on some of the basic positions that the coalition partners will support. It is clear that whatever promises a coalition party might make, they are not likely to deliver them to the citizens because too many interests clash within their coalition and there is the continuous opposition of the losing parties.

The U.S. political party system is much simpler with two durable parties, the Republicans and the Democrats. The Republicans represent mostly the interests of business and the wealthy. They claim to be the party that will produce the most economic growth and this will 'trickle down' to the less fortunate. Actually more economic growth has occurred when the Democrats were in power and there was more 'trickle down' because of passing more social benefit programs. The Democrats represent mostly the interests of the working and middle classes. The Republicans used to claim to serve the middle class but they are losing their hold because the American middle class is shrinking. The Great Recession starting in 2008 depressed the middle class size, wages and net worth. In 2012, the middle class stood at 51% of the American population, down from 61% of 1971.

There have been occasional minor parties such as the Bull-Moose Party with Teddy Roosevelt, the Socialist Party with Norman Thomas, and America's First Party, inspired by Pat Buchanan. But none of these parties have gone far or lasted long. Sometimes a well-known person such as Ralph Nader or H. Ross Perot decides to run and their number of votes, although small, can often shift victory to the opposing party. Had Ralph Nader not run in 2000, Al Gore would have clearly won the Democratic Election that year.

One could argue that a permanent third party in the U.S. would confer some benefits. First, the voters would have a choice between three candidates instead of only two candidates. Second, the third party might be more moderate than the two parties that might have become polarized. In the U.K. for example, the Liberal Democrats, although rarely in power, are seen as occupying the 'center ground' between Labour on the Left and the Conservatives to the Right. Third, the two major parties will be influenced in their choice of policies by the policies advertised by the third party.

In years past, U.S. parties were cordial to one another and certain leaders in one party, such as Democratic leader Ted Kennedy and Republican John McCain, enjoyed high respect by members of the other party. Some bills were jointly sponsored by a member from each party. Both parties respected the need to compromise and find solutions if possible, especially if both could claim a win-win.

HOW THE PARTIES DIFFER: POLARIZATION AND GRIDLOCK?

How much has changed since those times! Since Obama's election in 2008 the two U.S. parties have become more polarized and gridlocked. We hear reports of stalemates and failed grand bargains. The Congress can't seem to pass any legislation. Let's examine three questions about polarization.

1. WHY IS THERE POLARIZATION?

The Republicans have started to move further to the Right in U.S. politics as a result of the growth of the activist Tea Party branch and other developments. The Tea Party has transmuted into the Freedom Caucus, consisting of about 40 House Republicans who are intransigent even within their own party. They will brook no compromise. They are willing to shut down the government if they can't have their way. In return for allowing the government to raise the debt ceiling, the Freedom Caucus wants major entitlement reforms, i.e., cuts to Social Security, Medicare, and Medicaid. They also demand the defunding of Planned Parenthood, the nuclear agreement with Iran, and Obamacare. They also will reject any omnibus spending bill so that they could fund the parts they like, such as the Department of Defense, while shutting down the parts they don't like, which is many agencies and bills. Along with Senate allies like Ted Cruz, they are trying to blackmail America into accepting their Far Right priorities. They don't want to let their positions be voted on Election Day because they know they would lose.

This led some Democrats to move further to the Left. It reached a point where the least conservative Republican was to the right of the most conservative Democrat. This is called *asymmetric polarization*. There is no overlap any more. The two sides are not just adversaries; they see the other side as the enemy. Norman Ornstein, an astute observer, says that the parties have settled into tribalism. The Republicans are anti-tax, also pro-life, pro-gun, and anti-marriage equality. Democrats who support a minimum-wage increase also support abortion rights and gay marriage.

The growing income gap in the U.S. causes candidates to rely more on extreme individual donors to influence their position. Also, party leaders are demanding and enforcing more party loyalty and discipline. The diversification and fragmentation of media and their growing partisanship in the news channels also contribute to more polarization. Voters increasingly select media either on television or the Internet to reinforce their views. Finally, there is less cross-aisle social interaction among Congress members. More members are spending more time out of Washington and in Washington their workloads are so heavy that little time is left for open informal exchange.

2. WHAT ARE THE CONSEQUENCES?

The increased ideological differences shrink the number of compromises that are possible. They increase the incentives for some members to engage in brinkmanship. The chance of a filibuster or a presidential veto reduce the chances of compromise. The Senate cannot close debate and finally vote without three-fifths of the Senate voting to do so. Some members of the Republican Party periodically threaten to close down government rather than compromise.

A 16-day shutdown occurred during October 1–16, 2013 because the Democrats would not agree to changes in Obamacare which were irrelevant to the real issue: Funding the government. The result was a government shutdown with approximately 800,000 federal employees indefinitely furloughed, and another 1.3 million required to report to work without known payment dates. The hit to U.S. taxpayers were in the multi-billions, not to mention all the hardship caused to so many citizens.

The real tragedy is that even if the Democrats win the presidential election, the new President cannot get anything done. This has led a number of voters to question why they should even vote, since it will make no difference in getting needed legislation. The Freedom Caucus completely emasculates the Madisonian constitutional imperative for bargaining and compromise.

3. WHAT ARE THE SOLUTIONS?

One solution is to reduce gerrymandering of Congressional districts that allow a Congressman or woman to win election after election and not face strong debate over his or her views. Another solution is to favor open primaries instead of running closed primaries usually attended by more extreme voters. A third solution is to improve campaign finance by reducing the influence of wealthy individual donors and PACs and Super PACs. A fourth solution is to change the rules regarding terminating debate, filibusters, and presidential vetoes.[2]

Only one in six Americans approve of how Congress is handling its job. There is excessive partisanship where each party works to get all of its members to vote the same way on whether the issue is raising the debt ceiling or expanding social security. The bipartisan coalitions of the past have given way to the party-line voting of the 21st Century.

America's two parties represent opposing ideologies. Republicans tend to evoke the glories of the past; they favor law and order, a strong military, rural values, religious values, and financial conservatism. Their mantra is smaller government and less regulation. They prefer to cut taxes and government costs and cut social and environmental benefits. They are anti-utopian and prefer the past and the present.

Consider the current policy positions taken by many Republicans:

- Abolish or greatly reduce Medicare and Medicaid.
- Reduce or eliminate Social Security.
- Terminate the Environment Protection Agency (EPA).
- Repeal minimum wage laws or leave them where they are.
- Replace today's income tax system with a single flat tax that everyone pays.
- Cut food stamps.
- Cut Head Start program for children.
- Cut housing assistance for poor families.
- Cut job training and employment assistance.
- Cut the budget for education.
- Defend the right of citizens to buy guns.
- Support the pro-life movement and ban abortions.

Although most Republicans are conservative in their economic, financial, and moral ideas, there are different wings in the Republican Party. One wing wants the U.S. to be tougher abroad by funding larger military budgets to attack ISIS and defend allies such as Ukraine. Another wing is more xenophobic and wants immigration rules to keep out people from other cultures that differ greatly. Another wing is strongly religious and wants to defend or expand the role of religion in our society. There are even a group of Republicans who are economically conservative but socially liberal, such as former New York City Mayor Michael Bloomberg. The economist Paul Krugman remains a strong critic of the Republican Party: 'The entire Republican Party is controlled by climate denialists, and anti-science types more broadly [...] the modern GOP is basically anti-rational analysis: it's at war not just with the welfare state but with the Enlightenment.'[3]

The Democrats care more about building a better future and they champion working people, civil rights, and big city values. Many Democratic Presidents use 'change' in their campaigns: Jimmy Carter's 'A Leader, for a Change' (1976); Bill Clinton's 'Change vs. More of the Same' (1992); and Barack Obama's 'Change You Can Believe In' (2008).[4] The Democrats typically endorse the following goals:

- Expand Social Security and Medicare and Medicaid and the Obama Plan.
- Invest in rebuilding infrastructure (roads, bridges, ports, etc.).
- Open up a path to citizenship for illegals who entered the country.
- Lower the cost of attending college by giving federal grants or building more low-cost community colleges.
- Eliminate egregious tax shelters and loopholes that lead high-income people to pay very low taxes or manage to avoid taxes altogether.
- Implement a higher progressive tax system on millionaires and billionaires.
- Implement a financial tax on financial securities transactions.
- Invest in a universal pre-Kindergarten program.
- Eliminate *Citizens United* that let companies, unions, associations, and individuals spend enormous amounts to win elections.

Likewise, the Democrats have different camps. We can distinguish between liberal Democrats and the progressive Democrats. Today Bernie Sanders and Elizabeth Warren represent the progressive wing of the Democratic Party, wanting the government to do even more, particularly to punish the banks for their role in the 2008 Financial Crisis, reduce government subsidies to businesses, drastically raise minimum wages, increase investment in environment and climate protection, increase investment in improving our infrastructure, pass a single-payer health system to replace Obamacare, and encourage more union growth to protect the interests of the working class. The more liberal wing of the Democratic Party is represented by Hillary Clinton, who is more pragmatic about what can be accomplished and more ready to get concessions from Republicans by compromising and trading on issues.

Still there remains a deep chasm between the two parties' vision of a Good Society. Politics has become a morality play. Polling data in 1960 showed that 5% of Republicans and Democrats said that they would be displeased if their child married someone from the other party. By 2010, 49% of Republicans and 33% of Democrats said that they would be displeased.[5]

Each party is intent on getting its members to vote for a different set of goals and values. Some extreme groups are in the party and the party needs their votes. The extremes are not ready to compromise. The hope is that some leaders in both parties don't subscribe wholeheartedly to these extreme groups and see the merit of getting something done even if it required compromising.

In the 2012 book by Norman Ornstein and Thomas Mann, *It's Even Worse Than It Looks*, the authors describe the new level of acrimony and dysfunction in Congress:

> The single-minded focus on scoring political points over solving problems, escalating over the last several decades, has reached a level of such intensity and bitterness that the government seems incapable of taking and sustaining public decisions responsive to the existential challenges facing the country [...] the country is squandering its economic future and putting itself at risk because of an inability to govern effectively.[6]

Each party needs to look ahead to imagine who its voters would be. The Republicans, in particular, might face an existential crisis. They are essentially an older white man's party working for the rich. They have less appeal than Democrats with women, African Americans, Hispanics, and Asians. Looking at the demographic trends of different groups, the Republicans are in danger of appealing to a lower share of voters, assuming that they don't soften some of their positions.

It is important to understand that parties are essential to the operation of a democracy. They represent a way of simplifying the complex and numerous issues encountered in a democracy. Most voters will know very little about most issues. Parties help simplify the complex political world into a set of position constellations. Citizen do not need to think deeply about individual issues but only vote for the party that supplies more of what they value. The citizen is comfortable in only having to vote for one party and not having to vote on hundreds of separate issues. Parties supply a solution to deep voter ignorance.

Once a party exists, its task is to raise money to allocate to its candidates and campaigns and build a strong image. It becomes a marketing and brand-building organization that adopts colors and mascots (the Republican elephant and the Democratic donkey) and choice phrases and values. It recruits workers and voters around its ideology and hopes to inflame them against the opposition and be ready to donate money and time to support new candidates and win the next elections.

How much money will the political parties spend on the 2016 U.S. election? In 2012, the Presidential and Congressional Elections cost a record $6.3 billion. It is estimated that the 2016 contest might run as high as $8 billion. This is partly because the *Citizens United* ruling by the Supreme Court allowed individuals and corporations to spend so much more than in the previous elections. The network run by the Koch brothers, whose members are not required to reveal their donors, has set a spending goal of nearly $900 million for the 2016 races, compared with $400 million in 2012. The question is whether all this money actually affects who we vote for. If it does, then Republican candidates will be favored to the extent that they collect more money from donors than the Democrats. If it doesn't, then both parties are wasting a lot of donor money that could have been put into better causes.

Today the electioneering system is carried on around the clock. As soon as the last election is finished, elected officials and other politicians start building their next campaign. The average citizen starts receiving campaign solicitations for small amounts—$3, $5, or more—related to one candidate or issue or another. If you are a Democrat, you are sure to get email solicitations from the likes of Al Franken, Nancy Pelosi, and others for money.

The most sensible solution to this heavy and continuation solicitation process is to pass a law that parties and candidates cannot solicit until a year before an election, or at least cannot start political advertising for two months before an election. Whatever a candidate has to say can be said in ads with sufficient repetition during a two-month period. This would reduce the amount being raised and spent on U.S. elections. This is the solution used in the U.K., and in their case 30 days are allowed for political advertising. But there is no way to stop them from giving speeches and building their campaign at a continuous nonstop pace.

Not everyone is satisfied with the two-party system in the U.S. Consider a person who is financially conservative but socially liberal. How is he or she to vote? More voters than ever are now describing themselves as an independent. Pew Research surveys in 2014 found that 39% of voters now identify as independents—more than the 32% who are Democrats and 23% who are Republicans. During polling and on Election Day, the choice is binary. The two major political parties are not likely to put out a candidate that many voters think is ideal. Often people will say they will not vote on Election Day either because neither candidate satisfies them or both candidates are too similar and it doesn't matter who wins.

The Super PACs are growing stronger today. They operate outside of the party system and consist of super-donors who favor their own candidates. They weaken the two parties. Taegan Goddard sees a time when each candidate's campaign is handled by a Super PAC.[7] He can imagine a Super PAC sponsoring a 'millennial-friendly, libertarian-lite candidate who was liberal on social issues, dovish on foreign policy, and conservative on economics.' This candidate would never be nominated by a major party but he is unbundled in a way that enough people might find him appealing. Imagine ten Super PACs backing ten ideologically diverse candidates. This would give the voters much more choice to find a favorite candidate. Finally, the voter is not forced into a two-person choice. The only downside is that the candidate will be very beholden to those supplying the money to the sponsoring Super PAC.

THE INFLUENCE OF POLITICAL ADVERTISING

A candidate and his or her managers strive to bring as much attention to the candidate as possible. In previous times, the number of possible exposure venues was limited. Before radio and television, the candidate would get exposure through appearing at home gatherings, picnics, and rallies. The candidate would smile, kiss babies, and give a short but hopefully inspiring speech replete with lots of patriotic rhetoric but little substance. The candidate's backers would fill newspapers and magazines with articles and reports of his or her speeches and favorable comments from others.

When radio and television came along, each candidate would hire one or more advertising agencies to prepare broadcast and video ads. The candidate would make a statement promising good times and normally put down the other party and its candidate. The candidates would use exaggeration and not hesitate at times to misquote facts. The ad would mention where viewers and fans could send their money to support the candidate.

Television arrived and played a major role in showing the candidate speaking or meeting with others and giving statements to the press. Many candidates went to school to learn how to talk to journalists and how to manage their appearance before the TV camera. The candidate needed to decide whether to wear a suit and tie or an open shirt, and maybe even jeans. Everything became an exercise in image management.

Hillary Clinton in 2015 went to Iowa and instead of initially giving speeches to large audiences, she sat down and talked to small groups of voters to learn what they thought about issues and then she would share her views. It was months before she announced policies that she would espouse. Then she released her campaign themes: Increased taxes on the wealthy, higher federal minimum wage, more government spending on infrastructure projects, new child care benefits, federal subsidies for college tuition, and laws to help expand unions.[8]

The arrival of the Internet and mobile phones expanded the opportunities for candidates to be seen and heard. A citizen could look up hundreds of articles mentioning the candidate or listen to or view a large number of videos featuring the candidate. Nothing is hidden from view, including the views of critics and opponents of the candidate. The candidate can also use the Internet to raise money for the campaign. Often an ad might appear on screen citing a disturbing issue or development and asking viewers to send $5 or more to help pay for a new ad or statement that would be sent to other viewers or Congress itself.

The job of each advertising agency is not only to build the candidate's image through many media such as film, print ads, magazine stories, email, talk shows, and appearances at events and rallies, but also to measure the exposure's impact. Did it switch any voters? Did it get them to talk favorably to others about the candidate? Did it increase the probability that the viewers would vote on Election Day? The agency would search for the types of exposure that would deliver the most positive impact. The more agency personnel would learn about this, the better they could justify the money spent.

CONCLUSION

From its beginning, Americans voted for preserving state rights and local control. The framers were careful to specify and limit the powers of the federal government. Yet it was necessary to knit the different states together to promote interstate commerce and set up common standards. The federal government is the agency in charge of pushing for common standards.

Nevertheless, there are many factions who distrust the federal government. The Tea Party and other anti-government groups think the federal government has become too big, unresponsive, regulatory, and wasteful. The Republican Party is continuously trying to compress the federal government's size and powers. Republicans hate federal deficits and grants to the needier citizens, sometimes thinking of them as lazy and taking advantage of good hard-working Americans.

The gridlock undertaken by the two parties over the last 20 years has had tragic consequences. Congress has not been dealing with or resolving major issues such as the growing inequality of income and wealth, the deteriorating physical infrastructure, the persistence of poverty, the inadequate attention given to climate change, the high burden in borrowing money to get a college education, and many other issues. It is no wonder that Congress continues to get one of the lowest ratings of all professional jobs. The Irish political philosopher Edmund

Burke stated: 'The only thing necessary for the triumph of evil is for good men to do nothing.'[9]

Americans can only hope that some Congress members have the courage to depart from their party's discipline and go across the aisle to work on a bill with a member from the other party. For example, Senator Elizabeth Warren (Democrat) will work with John McCain (Republican) to restore the Glass-Steagall Act that separates commercial banking from investment banking. The intent is to prevent banks from becoming so large that we cannot let them fail. This may be a sign that both parties may once again start working with each other to improve the state of the nation.

NOTES

1   See: http://en.wikipedia.org/wiki/List_of_political_parties_in_Italy (accessed 03.03.16).

2   See M. Barber and N. McCarty, 'Causes and Consequences of Polarization': www.apsanet.org/Files/Task%20Force%20Reports/Chapter2Mansbridge.pdf. Also, see M. Golden, 'Unlock Congress: Reform the Rules—Restore the System' (Why Not Books, Pacific Grove, CA, 2015) (accessed 03.03.16).

3   Paul Krugman, "Fear of Asymmetry," *New York Times,* August 28, 2015.

4   U.S. Chamber of Commerce, 'The Tattooed and Pierced Longhairs Never Showed Up', March 18, 2013, pp. 26–30.

5   D. Brooks, 'Why Partyism is Wrong', *New York Times*, October 27, 2014.

6   N. Ornstein and T. Mann, *It's Even Worse Than It Looks: How the American Constitutional System Collided with the New Politics of Extremism* (Basic Books, New York, 2013).

7   T. Goddard, 'Can America's Politics be Unbundled from America's Political Parties?', *The Week*, April 27, 2015.

8   See: www.washingtontimes.com/news/2015/jul/12/carly-fiorina-rips-hillary-clintons-big-government/#ixzz3fij6zfXN (accessed 03.03.16).

9   http://www.goodreads.com/quotes/370-the-only-thing-necessary-for-the-triumph-of-evil-is

CHAPTER 8

REFORMING FOREIGN POLICY MAKING—WHO SHOULD MAKE FOREIGN POLICY?

'The purpose of foreign policy is not to provide an outlet for our own sentiments of hope or indignation; it is to shape real events in a real world.'

John F. Kennedy

Early in American history, many Americans preferred isolationism, not getting involved with the rest of the world. There was plenty of work and opportunity to build the American nation without paying attention or getting involved in foreign affairs. Yes, doing trade abroad with other countries was necessary and profitable. But getting entangled in their plots and wars was unwise.

But events and opportunities in the last century propelled the U.S. into becoming the most powerful nation in the world. The 19th Century was Britain's century and the 20th Century was America's century. America came to the aid of other countries in World War I and World War II and its victories established its leadership of the free world. The United Nations was established in New York City after World War II in the hope of preventing future world wars.

Then the country was drawn into the Korean War (1950–1953) followed by the Vietnam War (1955–1975). On August 2, 1990, President George H. W. Bush rushed to aid Kuwait against Saddam Hussein's invasion and the Gulf War ended quickly on February 28, 1991. On March 20, 2003, George W. Bush appeared on television and gave a four-minute speech: 'My fellow Americans, at this hour, American and coalition forces are in the early stages of military operations to disarm Iraq, to free its people and to defend the world from grave danger.' On May 1, 2003, Bush declared 'Mission Accomplished' and major Iraq combat operations were over. However, it was not until December 13 that coalition forces captured Saddam Hussein.

George W. Bush gave 'weapons of mass destruction' as his reason for attacking Iraq. This was later exposed as a fiction. As the Iraq War progressed, Bush said that America's aim was to bring democracy into the Middle East. America became further involved in the Middle East with the invasion into Afghanistan in 2001. The Afghanistan War did not go well and President Obama started withdrawing in 2014.

On December 17, 2010, with Mohamed Bouazizi's self-immolation in Tunisia, the Arab Spring protests began in Tunisia, Egypt, Libya, Yemen, Syria, and Bahrain. Instead of bringing freedom and democracy, most of these uprisings were crushed and ended with military rule.

All of these developments raise the question, 'What should America's foreign policy be and who is to guide it for the next century?'

VIEWING U.S. FOREIGN POLICY ABROAD

The U.S. government needs to define the role it is to play in different parts of the world. For a long time America was the only superpower, leading the world in military and commercial might. It needed to keep the world orderly and free of war. That way its trade would be successful and it could promote its ideas of capitalism and democracy. Often, however, America was dragged into taking a stand and defending some countries or regions. In 1983, President Ronald Reagan called the USSR the 'Evil Empire' and the U.S. conducted a long drawn out Cold War that raged in different parts of the world. These were the only two nations armed with nuclear weapons, and fortunately the two enemies never went to 'brinkmanship.' The U.S. had the ability to outspend the Soviet Union, and the latter finally caved in.

Then in 2002, President George W. Bush gave a speech calling North Korea, Iran, and Iraq the 'Axis of Evil.' The U.S. entered Iraq to get rid of Saddam Hussein and spent $3 trillion dollars, according to Joseph Stiglitz in *The Three Trillion Dollar War*, not counting a total of 4,491 U.S. service members killed and tens of thousands badly wounded or injured. Having learned no lesson, America went into Afghanistan and realized soon enough that nothing would be accomplished. President Obama quite rightly arranged a withdrawal, knowing that no military solution would settle problems in the Middle East. The problems aren't over because of the rise of ISIS and the continuation of terrorism.

President Obama may make military moves deemed necessary (such as drone strikes and air attacks) without needing Congressional approval. He always has to face a strong, usually Republican group that pushes for military action. Yet his course is to favor diplomacy over warfare and to work with close allies who participate in joint strategic decision making. He has to work hard to convince both parties and the public that a particular foreign policy stance makes sense. This is even more difficult because of the normal secrecy that envelops foreign commitments and issues and prevents most people from knowing the deeper issues. Here it is worth noting John F. Kennedy's words of warning that, 'Domestic policy can only defeat us; foreign policy can kill us.'

Today the U.S. is no longer the only superpower. There is China and Russia, and a number of other potential superpowers including India, Brazil, Turkey, and Indonesia. Continuing to be the world's policeman is economically impossible and not favored by many Americans. This raises the question of what is America's basic purpose in the world. Is it to keep peace and order in the world so that countries can prosper through active global trade? Is it to prevent some 'bad' nations from harming their people or other peoples? Is it to liberate or save other nations as has been done in the past? Is it to set an example at home for what real democracy and capitalism are like so that other nations can emulate them? Or is it to withdraw from interfering with other nations and focus on building America's own future with fewer foreign entanglements? There are many competing opinions about these possibilities.

The task boils down to define U.S. foreign policy in each major area of the world. Let us review U.S. current policy in the major continents.

ASIA

The U.S. is centering its attention on Asia aware of the talk that the 21st Century will be the Chinese century. The populations of China, India, Indonesia, and Japan account for almost one-quarter of the world's population. China is the current focus and the world is impressed with its accomplishments, including in the past 30 years lifting the largest number of people out of poverty, acting as the world's factory, buying up great amounts of raw materials from Asia and Africa, setting up major trade partnerships, and moving slowly from low-price, low-quality goods to improved products and services. China boasts a new horde of billionaires and millionaires aided by a fairly free capitalistic system headed by a benign one-party authoritarian government that can get things done fast and well, including trains running at 124 miles per hour, new dams being built to redirect the flow of rivers, and plans to build at least another ten mega-cities. China has already passed Japan and now ranks as the world's second largest economy. It has by and large been on an expansion course. It is reclaiming some islands off of China and building its naval power. China has some unhappy Muslim groups in the Southeast and there are tensions between different Chinese groups who may want to claim separate nation territory.

China is currently facing a weakening economy. Its finances are hurting. It has expanded too fast. It is selling less abroad and buying less abroad, much to the injury of some emerging countries who gained while China was growing. China is focusing on growing its domestic market. But Chinese wage earners, who don't get paid much, still try to save half of their earnings for retirement or a 'rainy day.' Furthermore, some Chinese companies are failing and closing down, causing an increase in the number of unemployed citizens.

What is the U.S. policy toward China? Essentially, it is containment. China is currently claiming ownership of some islands in the hands of other countries, it makes sure to continue controlling Tibet, and it is always considering whether to take over Taiwan. While carrying on superficially friendly relations with China's leaders, at the same time the U.S. is building allies in Japan, South Korea, Indonesia, India, and the Philippines to act as a surrounding system to contain China. China is fully aware of this and continues to invest in building its military system partly as a reaction. The irony is that China has done a good job for its people and there is every reason that the U.S. needs to remain friendly to the Chinese people.

India is the second power in Asia and the U.S. is very friendly and trade-active in India. It lies in the U.S. interest that India keeps investing in infrastructure and improving the lives of its people. Prime Minister Modi is a benign and talented leader who wants a good relationship with the U.S. As a long-standing democracy, the interests of India and the U.S. are very in sync. As India prospers, the U.S. will benefit from India's market growth.

Both Japan and Indonesia are friendly countries under strong leaders who are happy to cooperate with the U.S., especially in preventing any aggressive moves by China. In Japan, Prime Minister Abe is pushing for a constitutional change that will allow Japan to invest in a military build-up. The U.S. is actively seeking trade agreements with many Asian countries to somewhat limit China's preeminent trade strength. The U.S. is clearly facing a delicate task of being pro-China in its trade relations but seeking to slow down China's economic and military steps.

THE MIDDLE EAST

The U.S. has fought costly wars in Iraq and Afghanistan only to find that these are troubled, somewhat artificial countries made up of many tribes and many splintered Muslim groups. Iraq is an artificial 'state' made up of many 'nations' that dislike each other and are frequently at war. The same can be said of Afghanistan and other states created by the Europeans when colonizing the Middle East.

If any lesson has been learned, it is that the Middle East is not ready for democracy and will continue to be ravaged in wars that will not have any winners. A Middle Eastern nation is likely to be best governed by a strong leader rather than a democratic process. President Obama has to carefully balance the interests of America's ally, Saudi Arabia, without giving too many concessions to the Saudi's religious and political enemy, Iran. Iran leads the Shi'a branch of Islam while Saudi Arabia leads the Sunni branch, and both are preparing their defenses.

Saudi Arabia became America's main ally when the U.S. needed Middle East peace largely to insure a steady supply of oil. This still remains the case, but America's dependence on oil has diminished greatly and ultimately the world will need less oil as oil and gas are found elsewhere and as cars become more electric and even driverless.

The U.S. is engaged in getting Iran to stop its ambition to build nuclear warheads and has reduced its boycott of Iran. But this means Iran's economy will grow faster and have more resources to release to Hezbollah and other terrorist groups that endanger Israel. So the U.S. needs a foreign policy that balances its interests in Saudi Arabia, Iran, and Israel, alongside terrible problems that are regularly occurring in Syria and Yemen. The U.S. decided not to send troops to Syria and originally worked against the interests of the Syrian government until ISIS formed as a new expanding power in the Middle East that required even more effort at containment. Now ISIS has taken over a good part of Iraq. The U.S. has decided not to send ground troops but to conduct air warfare against ISIS, hoping that Iraq's soldiers might fight back with more support from the U.S. The worst fear is that ISIS may take over Pakistan and have access to its nuclear weapons.

Many conservatives in the Republican Party have condemned Obama's resistance to putting troops on the ground and see the U.S. as losing more influence in the area. Obama has made it clear that there is no such thing as victory in the Middle East and that no American blood should be spilled in this troubled area.

Recently he has agreed to send more special operations soldiers to Iraq to help fortify the military situation.

The other Middle Eastern acute problem is the conflict between Palestine and Israel. Palestinians in Gaza and in the West Bank say that Israel is an occupier and the Palestinian people have a right to rebel and even bomb Israel to get back their lands. Israel is not going to give back any land as long as the Palestinian people pledge to destroy Israel. American Presidents before and since Bill Clinton have invested great energy in trying to bring the two sides together and use third parties to collaborate in finding and proposing solutions. The Middle East will remain a major concern faced by American Presidents and all Western leaders of the future.

EUROPE

Europe remains a solid ally of the U.S. based on a long history of trade, shared democracy, and mutual interest. The U.S. is on excellent terms with the U.K. and Germany and has good relations with Scandinavian countries, and southern and eastern European countries. Unfortunately, Europe's economies have grown only slowly. Europe has high unemployment (28% in Greece and 22% in Spain) and its countries are saddled with high welfare costs. Europe's southern 'PIGS' countries (Portugal, Italy, Greece, and Spain) have all experienced negative growth of late. Greece is the major case facing whether it will go bankrupt and exit the eurozone or continue to be subsidized. Europe is concerned about the repercussions of a Greek euro failure that might cascade.

The U.S. main foreign policy issue in Europe is containing the influence of Russia under President Putin. Russia has already expanded into Crimea, which was part of Ukraine. Putin says that Russian citizens living in eastern Ukraine are claiming rights to parts of Ukraine. Russia is attempting to build its own set of allies and act as a thought leader in Europe by objecting to many of the liberal leanings of Europe. Russia uses every opportunity to show its military might in parades so that Europe doesn't make any wrong moves. Putin is putting more of Russia's scarce resources into building its military power and it has developed some of the most advanced rockets and submarines. Russia feels endangered by the nuclear shield that the U.S. is placing at various points in Europe ostensibly to protect European countries against a Russian attack. Current and future U.S. Presidents will have to decide how much military help to give to Ukraine and the Baltic countries without getting into a new Cold War with Russia.

Today a major concern in Europe, a historically Christian continent, is the growing Muslim population as more and more refugees flee the Middle East and North African countries looking for a better life free from war and military dictatorships. Europe has tried to slow down the hordes of migrants and asylum seekers from reaching Europe via boats and illegal human trafficking because of political, economic, and cultural implications. Some think that Europe's fate as a future Muslim continent has already been sealed, given the large Muslim populations in Germany, Sweden, and elsewhere, as well as the higher birthrates among Muslims. Europeans wonder if their age-old traditions and practices will vanish. The U.S. sees this largely as Europe's problem because it cannot take sides and still satisfy its Middle Eastern allies.

AFRICA

Africa started out as a dark continent where only some Europeans sailed around its perimeter. Then an increasing number of explorers from Britain, France, Germany, the Netherlands, and Belgium started to penetrate the hinterland and lay claims to territory. In a relatively short period, most of Africa was cut up into European colonies. Britain carved a vertical slice all the way from Egypt in the north to South Africa in the south. France cut its vertical slice mostly in West Africa to include Algeria, Morocco, Tunisia, and other countries.

There is wide agreement that Africa will become a superpower of the future, especially if it can secure strong leadership in its leading countries such as Egypt, Nigeria, and Kenya. Africa consists of 26 countries with varying levels of economic development and many internal problems and border clashes. Africa is extremely rich in minerals and agricultural resources and China has been putting capital and its people to work in Africa. Global businesses wanting to lower their costs of production, especially in labor-intensive industries, would do well to move production to Africa.

The U.S. has not been heavily involved in Africa except to use soft power to help abet clashes within and between African countries. The U.S. has been generous in giving foreign aid to Africa. But many have criticized how little of the foreign aid actually reaches the poor; one estimate is 15% of the money given. One cynic defined foreign aid as 'a transfer of money from poor people in rich countries to rich people in poor countries.'[1] The U.S. doesn't yet see Africa as a major market for its goods and services because of its poverty, its political corruption, and uncertainties. It would make sense for the U.S. to think more deeply about choosing the right African allies and preparing for African prosperity as Africa grows stronger.

SOUTH AND CENTRAL AMERICA

The U.S. government too often neglects paying sufficient attention to its neighbors to the south. Mexico has been growing as an economy ever since the Free Trade Agreements (FTA) were struck. Brazil, one of the 'BRIC' nations (Brazil, Russia, India, and China), is a sizeable power that can have a great influence on the economies and economic development of other South American countries. Chile and Colombia run successful economies. However, a few South American countries continue to take a Marxist approach to growth, led by Venezuela when it was being ruled by Hugo Chávez. He influenced Bolivia, Paraguay, and Ecuador to align with Cuba and other Marxist states. Today, however, Venezuela is a skeleton of its former self now that its leader is gone and its economy shattered. Problems still haunt Central America, including Haiti, Guatemala, and Honduras, with Costa Rica, Nicaragua, Panama, and the Dominican Republic in much better condition.

HOW IS U.S. FOREIGN POLICY MADE?

It is clear that future U.S. Presidents will have their hands full in sorting out problems with other countries. They will have to decide who will be their allies, who will be neutral, and who will be their enemies. Isolationism is not possible. Foreign countries will grow their economic strength and wield their military power. The U.S. must protect its electricity grid that could easily be hacked. The U.S. government and American companies must invest in security systems to protect their information from being hacked by cyber attacks.

U.S. foreign policy is in the hands of the U.S. President and can shift every time a new President takes power. One of the most important posts is the State Department, which has been led in recent times by Madeleine Albright, Colin Powell, Condoleezza Rice, Hillary Clinton, and John Kerry. Each successive Secretary of State reports to the President and carries out his or her policies. The State Department is a huge bureaucracy with experts covering every country in the world and who are networked with tens of thousands of foreign experts and sources.

The U.S. Constitution divides foreign policy powers between the President and Congress. Each share in the making of foreign policy. Both branches can initiate and change foreign policy. Making and defending foreign policy is a complex process.[2]

The President and the State Department can make foreign policy through the way it responds to foreign events, or negotiates international agreements, through releasing policy statements and proposals for legislation. Congress can either support the President's approach or seek to change it. When foreign policy changes occur through presidential action, it is difficult to change in the short term because it takes time for Congress to react. Often Congress receives proposals from the executive branch on treaties and international agreement where the Senate or Congress must approve. In most cases Congress approves, often after making significant modifications to the President's initial proposal.

On the other hand, Congress can initiate foreign policy through resolutions and policy statements, legislative directives, legislative pressure, informal advice, or funding denials. The executive branch can support or try to change congressional policies as it sees its interest and the public's interest.

As a result, it is difficult to decide who should be credited with any foreign policy because it evolved out of the shared work of both branches. Foreign policy is not in the form of a grand design but rather is the result of much compromising of individual policies occurring in different countries and regions. It is true that at times the President is a strong leader in foreign policy and at other times Congress has been dominant.

CONCLUSION

The U.S. has no choice but to be continuously involved in the affairs of other nations. Things can happen at home and abroad—financial crises, nuclear buildups, cyber attacks—that can greatly affect the lives of Americans. The U.S. will inevitably be drawn into siding with its traditional partners and their concerns.

The best posturing for the U.S. is to work hard for peace and prosperity everywhere in the world. It should continue to push for more globalization and trade. When countries become dependent on their trade partners, they are less likely to go to war. The U.S. should prefer diplomatic solutions to emerging problems. It should seek to strengthen the United Nations as a world body to adjudicate issues fairly and quickly. It should support the World Bank and the International Monetary Fund as important financial and economic support systems. It should favor the growth of regional trade organizations that will develop mechanisms of joint planning and adjudication within their region.

NOTES

1   Ephraim Hardcastle, 'Foreign aid: "Poor people in rich countries sending money to rich people in poor countries,"' *Daily Mail*, July 2, 2010.
2   See: 'Foreign Policy Roles of the President and Congress', June 1, 1999. U.S. Department of State: http://fpc.state.gov/6172.htm (accessed 03.03.16).

CHAPTER 9

REFORMING GOVERNMENT SERVICE—ARE GOVERNMENT EMPLOYEES EFFICIENT AND CONSCIOUS THAT THEY ARE 'PUBLIC SERVANTS'?

'We must remember not to judge any public servant by any one act.'
Theodore Roosevelt

Citizens vary in the degree that they feel that public agencies and public employees are serving them well. At one extreme are citizens who are voluble in their dislike of government. They say that government is too big, too inefficient, and too regulatory of our lives. They complain about taxes. They characterize public employees as lazy, poorly trained, and overpaid. At the other extreme are citizens who want government to grow larger and do more work to fix common problems. They want government to fix deteriorating infrastructure, improve weak primary and secondary schools, improve the health system, ensure food supply is safe, and penalize companies that create environmental hazards.

The majority of citizens don't make a judgment about government as a whole but like certain features of government and dislike others. They like good roads and bridges, a good electric grid, a good supply of water, and competent teachers, police, and firefighters. On the other hand, they dislike standing in a long line to renew a license or to vote or to deal with a public employee who is unhelpful or acts imperiously.

Citizens carry a different view of the federal government, state government, city government, and even neighborhood government. Although Americans mostly talk about the operations of the federal government, they also need to be cognizant of the views and expectations of local and regional governments.

One of the major problems with government is the presence of 'red tape.' Red tape has come to connote the worst of bureaucracy: Cynically impersonal service, bound up in meaningless paperwork, and beset by excessive, duplicative, and unnecessary procedures.[1] Red tape is not exclusive to government services. It is also found in large organizations and even in smaller nonprofit organizations.

Much of the experience that people have with government agencies is affected by the quality of their personnel. Civil service tests were established so that persons seeking a career in government would need to have the necessary knowledge to carry on their work and help citizens. The hope is that government organizations will emulate business organizations in emphasizing efficiency, good customer relations, problem solving ability, and empathy.

The heads of government agencies need to be 'servant leaders' who show a caring attitude toward their clientele that hopefully will be copied by their staff. Whereas companies can use incentives to drive better staff behavior (bonuses, promotions, etc.), government organizations have less scope for using incentives to drive the desired staff behavior. Companies can rely on competitors to keep their staff working hard but many government agencies are monopolies without competitors. To insure good staff behavior, government agencies need to collect feedback from citizens on how staff members carried out their duties. Still it is harder for government agencies to get rid of poor performers than it is for companies.

IMPROVING CITIZEN SERVICE IN THE PUBLIC SECTOR[2]

Customer satisfaction levels will have an effect on the revenues of government agencies, especially where citizens have choices for where to go for products, programs, and services.

Consider public transportation. A community transit system has tough competition from America's 'love affair' with the car and its convenience. Whether a citizen will give up his or her car and use public transportation will be highly correlated with the satisfaction with schedules, routes, numbers of transfers needed, timeliness, courtesy of the driver, cleanliness of the bus (and its riders), location of stops, whether there are shelters for waiting, even whether there are benches to sit on while waiting. Perceptions and experience of these aspects of the offer will impact the agency's annual revenues. Improving public service and satisfaction will increase future funding.

Consider another example. In April 21, 2005, a headline in the *Seattle Times* warned '10 Seattle Schools Targeted for Closure. Sweeping changes aimed at trimming deficit.' Reading on, the article explains that the district is faced with a growing budget gap and years of declining enrollment, in part due to birthrate declines but also impacted by families choosing private schools or moving to the suburbs. Since school districts are funded based on enrollment, the declining enrollment meant the district needed to drastically reduce its budget and was considering school closures and consolidations to reduce operating costs.

For agencies such as school districts that rely on government subsidies, customer satisfaction will have an impact. Levels of satisfaction with schools will be based on everything from classroom size, to how far a child is bussed (or not), to special offerings such as advanced science classes, to how administrators and their staff respond to parent and student concerns. When expectations are not met, parents consider other choices to fill their unmet needs including private schools or moving to the suburbs or a different school district.

Consider still another example. The U.S. Farmers Market Nutrition Program aims to increase the use of fresh, locally grown fruits and vegetables. It is funded by federal and local matching funds. Eligible recipients are issued coupons that can be redeemed only for fresh fruits and vegetables and herbs at farmers' markets. Whether families go to the farmers' market and use their coupons will depend on a number of variables including perceived convenience of transportation and parking, choices of produce, and how they are treated when they offer farmers their coupon instead of cash. Redemption levels will be reported and will affect future funding.

IMPROVING OPERATIONAL PERFORMANCE

Customers appreciate the benefits of increased operational efficiencies, often resulting in outcomes such as shorter lines, minimal waiting time and hassle-free experiences. The agency also benefits from these conditions, having to expend fewer resources delivering service. The key to success is to design, monitor, and adjust processes and procedures based on customer needs, preferences, and behaviors. It requires an ongoing commitment to a cycle of feedback and adjustments.

Consider the troublesome problem of airport security lines and what airports and their employees have done to speed up the process. Each adjustment and enhancement is rooted in an understanding of the customer's comfort and motivations. Providing a plastic bag for pocket change and keys at the beginning of the line motivates passengers to empty their pockets faster. Lines are cued and curved, recognizing time savings if passengers can be readily directed to the next available checkpoint. Signage with icons prohibiting the carry-on of certain items are helpful. So are signs that laptops must be removed before reaching the conveyor belt. The security agent provides a final reminder to remove one's shoes. This way the system works better and passengers experience a shorter wait and are even more prepared the next time. Satisfaction then reinforces behaviors and continues to increase the agency's operational efficiency.

Similar concepts are applied to community health clinics seeking greater efficiencies. The aim is to help patients keep appointments, arrive on time with any important records or information and to then follow recommended treatment plans. A reminder call or card increases chances of keeping the appointment and bringing along important items. When patients are seen at their appointed arrival time, it increases the chances they will arrive on time for their next appointment. To increase compliance with treatment plans, follow-up treatment calls and visits provide increased motivation and reinforcement.

Many government agencies develop performance measures to determine priorities for the future. Consider the following example. The U.S. Census Bureau recognizes the need for customer satisfaction to help the Bureau reach its performance goals. In the Bureau's 2004–2008 Strategic Plan, one goal is most relevant: '*Strategic Goal 1*: Meet the needs of policymakers, businesses and nonprofit organizations, and the public for current measures of the U.S. population, economy and governments.'[3] This goal is supported by several objectives, with one most applicable to customer satisfaction: '*Objective 1.3*: Ease the reporting burden on respondents.' It is recognized by the agency that successful data collection depends on the cooperation of those who provide the data—individuals, families, businesses, and governments—and that minimizing the reporting burden on respondents will increase their cooperation and decrease operational costs.

The U.S. Census Bureau uses the following steps to improve performance:

- Facilitate and simplify reporting by expanding electronic reporting capabilities and options, such as responding to recurring surveys via electronic means.
- Use respondent-centered approaches to data collection to facilitate participation and ease response.

- Align data collection procedures with the record-keeping practices of households and businesses to encourage participation.
- Take full advantage of federal, state, and private sector information to eliminate redundant data requests.

Performance is measured, in part, by return rates. For the Census 2000, the final mail return rate was 78.4%, an increase of over 3% from the final return rate in 1990 of 75%.[4]

PRACTICES TO DELIVER MORE CUSTOMER SATISFACTION

Here we describe five major practices utilized in the commercial sector that can also be used in the public sector.[5]

1. SUPPORT EMPLOYEES TO DELIVER GREAT SERVICE

Public sector employees, especially those on the frontline serving the customer, play a key role in the quality of delivered service. Consider:

- A policeman ticketing a driver.
- A librarian at a helpdesk.
- A child protective services case manager making a house call.
- An IRS staff member answering a hotline for questions.
- A teacher disciplining a student.
- An employment security counselor helping a teen with a job application.
- A director conducting a tour at a federal museum.
- An agent searching a passenger at an airport security checkpoint.

Each represent opportunities for creating satisfied customers, building loyalty, and engendering positive word of mouth—or not. Successful organizations have reversed the traditional organization chart, placing the customers at the top and frontline people, those who meet and serve customers, next. Middle managers are positioned to reflect the critical support they provide to frontline people so they can serve customers well. And at the base is top management, charged especially with hiring and supporting great managers (see Figure 9.1).

Given the importance of positive employee attitudes, service companies direct their attention and resources to attracting the best employees, developing sound

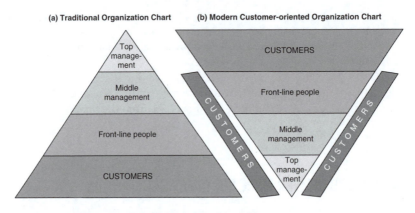

Figure 9.1   The Reverse Pyramid Organizational Chart

(but simple) training programs, and providing support and recognition for great performance.

Robert Spector has conducted extensive research on Nordstrom, the department store, and offers several recommendations for people on the frontline.[6] The following seem most relevant for public sector agencies:

- *Hire the Smile. Train the Skill.* 'We can hire nice people and teach them to sell, but we can't hire salespeople and teach them to be nice.'
- *Lead by Example.* The story is told of the manager of a department who one day spotted a can of pop on the counter. He just picked it up, put it in a wastebasket and then continued on his way. The employees witnessed this and they all got the message of keeping their area clean.
- *Empower Employees to Solve Problems to Satisfy the Customer.* When a citizen has a problem, the employee should not just say nothing can be done. Exceptional employees will go a step further and try to work with the customer to find a solution.
- *Celebrate Heroic Acts.* Recognize and showcase outstanding acts of customer service. This activity makes the recipient feel good and sends a clear message throughout the company that the way to advance is to give great customer service.

2. ENSURE INFRASTRUCTURES AND SYSTEMS HELP, NOT HINDER, SERVICE DELIVERY

Working in a well-functioning system is the key to excellent customer service. We know they affect a well-intended employee's ability to serve his or her customer. It is important to pinpoint contact points and procedures that should be explored for potential improvement. Consider the following two examples of improving the delivery system.

The Singapore government runs Singapore's Changi Airport. This airport has been recognized for numerous years as the best airport in the world.[7] Perhaps these outcomes are rooted in a vision of being the world's best airport and global air hub and, more importantly, a focus on providing speedy and hassle-free clearance, what many customers want most. It is reported that passengers take less than three minutes to clear immigration, claim their baggage and go through customs procedures. Departing passengers are said to find a similar convenience, expedited by a systems approach. One example of a technological improvement to their systems was the installation of a new software tool designed to simplify check-in, especially during peak travel periods.[8]

Consider 911, the emergency telephone number used in the U.S. Imagine the frustration and distraction for staff when the number is used for such calls as reporting lost pets, stolen bicycles, potholes, faulty street lights, and abandoned vehicles. Several cities are now offering an alternative for residents who have non-emergency calls, a 311 service. The intent is to improve responsiveness to citizens when they need information and to support callers by steering them in the right direction, making city government more efficient and effective and more like 'one-stop shopping' for its citizens.

3. CONSIDER OR ENHANCE CUSTOMER RELATIONSHIP MANAGEMENT SYSTEMS

Government agencies are increasingly turning to customer relationship management (CRM) systems to improve citizen satisfaction in the public sector. CRM systems include special software, sometimes hardware, that enables the organization to access and monitor real-time as well as historical detailed individual customer information. The architecture of a CRM system will include operational as well analytical components and will involve collaboration in order to capture customer data through the variety of customer contact points. Consider the following two examples.

In Queensland, Australia, the Child Safety and Disability Services department believes their new integrated client-management system will help it track and manage cases more effectively as youths move through the Courts and state-sponsored care programs. In the past, the department relied on faxes to exchange information with law-enforcement agencies and courts around the country, and that information was then manually entered into computers. This new system enables agencies to exchange client data electronically, with beneficial outcomes including more time for workers to spend with clients, which may mean kids are reintegrated into home environments more quickly.[9]

U.S. government spending on CRM systems has been growing largely due to the 1998 Government Paperwork Elimination Act that requires agencies to provide electronic options for paper-based processes, including transactions with customers such as bill payment. This spending is expected to be highest among civilian agencies that have large customer service transactions with extensive customer data, ones such as the Internal Revenue Service and the Social Security Administration.[10]

4. DISCOVER THE BENEFITS OF TOTAL QUALITY MANAGEMENT

Total Quality Management (TQM) was developed in the mid-1940s by Dr. W. Edwards Deming, who was known for his use and application of statistics to achieve quality at a reduced cost. One of his core concepts is that quality is defined by the customer and achieved through continuous improvement. Although Japanese manufacturing companies were among the first to adopt Dr. Deming's theories, he caught the attention of many American companies in the 1970s and 1980s and a few public sector agencies as well. Consider how the Mayor of Madison, Wisconsin, used Deming's concept of total quality improvement.[11]

While Mayor of Madison from 1983–1989, Joseph Sensenbrenner attended a presentation by Deming, who was 82 at the time. An early analogy presented by Deming struck home. It was his revolutionary (at the time) perspective that the potentially fatal flaw causing market share loss for U.S. companies was its system of 'make-and-inspect', which if applied to making toast would be expressed, 'You burn. I'll scrape.'[12] The critical issue Deming was referring to was that instead of correcting defects 'downstream', we needed to get our 'upstream' processes under control. And to do this, an organization must practice proven quality techniques and define this first as continuous improvement in pleasing customers.

An inspired Sensenbrenner began experimenting. His first stop was the city garage and his first daunting goal—to decrease vehicle repair turnaround time. He took it a 'Deming' step at a time. He first gathered data from individual mechanics and from the repair process itself. He found that many delays resulted from the garage not having the right parts in stock. The parts manager said the problem with stocking parts was that the city purchased many different makes and models of equipment virtually every year, estimating that the current fleet included 440 different types, makes, models, and years of equipment.

This was due to a city policy to buy whatever vehicle had the lowest sticker price on the day of purchase. The parts purchaser agreed with the mechanic that fewer parts to stock would make the job easier, but proclaimed that central purchasing wouldn't allow it. Central purchasing pointed the finger at the comptroller and the comptroller then pointed to the city attorney. At this apparent 'end of the road' moment, the city attorney replied that this was 'of course' possible and that all that was needed was (more) detailed written specifications in advance. In fact, he assumed they were doing that all along.

Sensenbrenner reported: 'The result of these changes was a reduction in the average vehicle turnaround time from nine days to three and a savings of $7.15 in downtime and repair for every $1 invested in preventive maintenance—an annual net savings to the city of Madison of about $700,000.'[13]

This first exercise confirmed for Sensenbrenner that the source of the slow turnaround was indeed upstream, one caused by a relationship of the city to its suppliers, not downstream where the worker couldn't find a missing part. It also confirmed that the Deming quality strategy was not simply a matter of adopting a new set of slogans or a new accounting system. It required teamwork and breaking down barriers between departments and involving employees in choosing the most cost-effective tools and materials for their jobs. And he found that employees were delighted that someone was listening to them instead of merely taking them to task.

MONITOR AND TRACK CUSTOMER EXPECTATIONS AND SATISFACTION LEVELS

One of the most important roles in an organization is to encourage and provide customer input and feedback. This information can provide insight on customer expectations, preferences, and needs to those designing programs and systems. They can measure and report on satisfaction (or not) with performance, and then make recommendations on areas for focus and on strategies for improvement.

One of the primary tools are periodic surveys. Using the findings from these surveys, managers gain perspectives on how citizens view and experience their services. The Institute for Citizen-Centered Service in Canada stresses that survey findings are most effective when they can be compared and evaluated against 'benchmarks' including expectations, goals, past performance, an industry standard, or the performance of peers.

One example of a benchmark initiative is The American Customer Satisfaction Index (ACSI), which tracks trends in customer satisfaction and provides insights for companies, industry trade associations, and government agencies. It is produced by the University of Michigan in partnership with the American Society for Quality and CFI Group, an international consulting firm. Having been selected in 1999 by the federal government to be a standard metric for measuring citizen satisfaction, over 60 federal government agencies have used the ACSI to measure citizen satisfaction of more than 100 services and programs.

Another measure that satisfaction (performance) scores might be compared with is perceived need or levels of concern with community or social issues. A city should ask a representative sample of citizens to rate the perceived importance of different problems facing the city. Then the city managers should compare this to their own list of ratings on importance. By considering both lists, city managers will have a better idea of what problems should receive the most attention in their budget.[14]

CONCLUSION

Through improved customer service and satisfaction, a government agency can experience multiple rewards including increased revenues, more support for future funding requests, enhanced operational efficiencies, and improved performance measures. Five major practices to assist in this include supporting employees to deliver great service, ensuring infrastructures and systems help (not hinder) service delivery, developing customer relationship management systems (CRM), employing total quality management (TQM) principles, and monitor and track customer expectations and satisfaction levels.

Managers in the public sector often complain about the difficulty of getting public employees to focus on creating customer value and satisfaction. The following examples show how public managers can promote a stronger customer focus.

To the person managing the 'only' building permit agency in town, we suggest that applying the TQM principles will make it more likely that your customers will complete your permit forms properly and accurately—the first time— saving you hassle and time and increasing your performance measures.

To the bus driver who questions the value of treating passengers like customers, we hope that a 'delighted' passenger might send a letter to your agency commending the driver and featuring the driver in the next employee newsletter, and even giving the driver a better schedule.

To those who don't see the benefit of letting customers 'have it their way,' one recognizes that schools could be closed due to declining satisfaction and enrollments.

To those who can't imagine how Amazon keeps track of customer data and history the way they do, check out a CRM system or software.

To those who don't believe public agencies have competition, ask the directors of your city's library or the local transit system what keeps them awake at night. For the librarian, it might be Google's databases, and for the transit director, Toyota's Prius.

And to those who don't understand 'all the fuss' about meeting expectations when expectations for government services are so low, we hope you now consider the good-news side of this equation. This should mean that it probably won't take much, then, to exceed expectations and by doing so you create opportunities for your agency to build loyal customers, enjoy positive word-of-mouth, maintain funding, increase revenues, and enjoy the status of a highly-regarded governmental agency.

NOTES

1   On red tape, see the opening chapter of B. Bozeman and M. K. Feeney, *Rules and Red Tape: A Prism for Public Administration Theory and Research* (Routledge, New York, 2015). A common definition of red tape is 'rules, regulations and procedures that require compliance but do not meet the organization's functional objective for the rule', (Barry Bozeman, *Bureaucracy and Red Tape*. Prentice-Hall, Englewood Cliffs, NJ, 2000).

2   Much of the rest of the chapter is adapted from Chapter 8 of P. Kotler and N. R. Lee, *Marketing in the Public Sector: A Roadmap for Improved Performance* (Wharton School Publishing, Philadelphia, PA, 2006).

3   U.S. Census Bureau, 2004–2008 Strategic Plan, *Strategic Goal 1*.

4   Census 2000 Mail Return Rates, January 30, 2003. Final Report USCENSUSBUREAU.

5   See R. Spector and P. D. McCarthy, *The Nordstrom Way to Customer Service Excellence: The Handbook for Becoming the 'Nordstrom of Your Industry'* (Wiley, Hoboken, NJ, 2012).

6   Spector and McCarthy, ibid.

7   Reported in Condé Nast *Traveler* magazine, by readers of the *Daily Telegraph* and the *Sunday Telegraph*, a UK newspaper, and the 'Top Overseas Airport' in Wanderlust Travel Awards among others.

8   Unisys, 'Singapore's Changi International Airport Services (CIAS) "Checking in" with New Unisys Solution to Expedite Passenger Processing.' www.ipress.com.hk/companyview.asp?id=9287 (accessed 16.05.16).

9   'Government Agencies Look to CRM Software', *Information Week*, December 6, 2004: http://informationweek.com/shared/printableArticleSrc.jhtml?articleID-54800256 (accessed 03.03.16).

10 'Feds Pump Up the CRM', *MM*, March/April, 2002, p.5.

11 J. Sensenbrenner, 'Quality Comes to City Hall', *Harvard Business Review*, March–April 1991.

12 Ibid., p.68.

13 Ibid., p.68.

14 N. Roberto, 'How to Make Local Governance Work', Asian Institute of Management, 2002.

CHAPTER 10

LEADING WITH VISION AND STATESMANSHIP—WHAT WILL IT TAKE TO RESTORE DEMOCRACY?

'A politician thinks of the next election. A statesman, of the next generation.'
James Freeman Clarke

The U.S. is admired by most of the world's countries for its standard of living, its progressive and democratic ideals, its interest in securing peace in the world, and the quality of its products and services. Countries respect America for its freedom of speech, the press and assembly, and rights that are badly missing in many other countries. They see America as a creative and innovative country developing new and better products and services to make life easier for more people.

Yet the U.S. also has domestic and foreign critics who level different complaints. Some say that the U.S. is too liberal in supporting such causes as abortion and same-sex marriage. They don't like its free talk about sex and allowing cartoons to mock the President, Islam, and others. Some charge the U.S. with coercing other countries mostly for the profit of the U.S. They say that the U.S. has too much power in the world and they want the U.S. to tame its power so that other power centers can operate.

Some countries are miffed by feeling relative neglect by the U.S. Many South American countries, including Mexico and Brazil, believe that the U.S. doesn't spend enough policy time thinking about these countries. The same is true for many African nations who feel they are suffering from benign neglect.

The fact is that the world has changed a lot in ways deeply emasculating the practice of democracy. Our citizens—the poor, the working class, the middle class, and the wealthy—have different goals and no group feels that any political party fully serves its interests. More decisions in the world are now influenced by multinational companies and by trade agreements beyond the control of the voters. Much legislation is the result of huge lobbying groups. Multinational companies obtain so much of their business abroad that they can even move much of their business to another country if they don't like the laws being passed in their own country. More of government itself is being privatized and less under the influence of the voters. The rich and super-rich have a disproportionate influence on the content of legislation.

THE FOURTEEN SHORTCOMINGS OF DEMOCRACY

In the first chapter of this book, I listed 14 shortcomings of democracy:

1 Low voter literacy, turnout, and engagement.
2 Shortage of highly qualified and visionary candidates.
3 Blind belief in American exceptionalism.
4 Growing public antipathy toward government.
5 Two-party gridlock preventing needed legislation.
6 Growing role of money in politics.
7 Gerrymandering empowering incumbents to get re-elected forever.
8 Caucuses and primaries leading candidates to adopt more extreme positions.
9 Continuous conflict between the President and Congress.
10 Continuous conflict between the federal and state governments.
11 The Supreme Court's readiness to revise legislative actions.
12 The difficulty of passing new amendments.
13 The difficulty of developing a sound foreign policy.
14 Making government agencies more accountable.

All of these shortcomings were discussed throughout the book, along with the proposed solutions. In this chapter we will re-examine each shortcoming and indicate the actions needed to remove or reduce each shortcoming.

1. LOW VOTER LITERACY, TURNOUT AND ENGAGEMENT

We noted that every four years, less than 55% of American citizens vote for who they want as the next President. It is even worse in the mid-term elections when less than 40% of the citizens vote for Representatives and Senators. Yet in several other industrial nations—Austria (75%), Belgium (89%), and Germany (71%)—the voting may get as high as 70–90%.

Libertarians could argue that citizens have the right *not* to vote. There is nothing in the Constitution requiring citizens to vote. They may have good reasons not to vote, such as no candidate addresses their interests, or it takes too much time, or it counts for too little. However, if we believe that more citizen voting and engagement in elections is desirable, here are some things that can be done:

- Make it easier to vote.
- Remove restrictions that require getting and showing an ID card.
- Make it easier to get to a polling station by locating more polling stations or keeping them open longer.
- Shift the election voting day to Saturday or Sunday or make Election Day a national holiday.
- Encourage more mail-in voting.
- Consider charging a fine to people who do not vote (as they do in Australia).
- Have more newspaper and radio and TV stations encouraging people to vote.
- Strengthen the teaching of civics in elementary schools, high schools and colleges.
- Automatically register all new 18-year-old citizens as having voting rights.

2. SHORTAGE OF HIGHLY QUALIFIED AND VISIONARY CANDIDATES

Many candidates in America's 50 states run each election period to be mayors, governors, Representatives, or Senators. The only requirement is that they be U.S. citizens. Yet running a city or a state or being a legislator requires a number of abilities. It would be desirable if citizens could be given information delivered through mass media of the knowledge and experiences of the individual candidates so that citizens can better judge their qualifications. Information would be supplied to questions such as: What should a would-be mayor know about budgeting, traffic planning, taxation, market research, business planning? What should a Congressional Representative know about how bills are passed? What should a presidential candidate know about bill passage, budgeting, vetoes, and foreign affairs to have a good grasp of the issues that he or she will face?

We are not saying that lacking 'job' knowledge would preclude anyone from running, only that voters might want to know more about a candidate's abilities to do the job. We need to encourage political scientists to sketch the knowledge and skills that individual political candidates need for various positions. Although a democracy is not to be confused with a meritocracy, we might wish that there would be more signs of merit.

We could get better-quality candidates if we raise the respect that we have for our elected politicians. As long as our elections are characterized by negative ad campaigning against opponents, many good people will choose not to run. As long as members of Congress have to vote their party line and not offer any compromising, the public will have a poor picture of politicians. We seem to have fewer politicians with the integrity and determination to correct our pressing problems. Instead we get many candidates who have low personal standards for integrity and whose real purpose is to pursue power, fame, or money in payment for their services.

We might have to go back to the idea of families or dynasties of candidates whose motives we can trust in that they are not after the money so much as to make things better for more people. However, this is not a recommendation.

3. BLIND BELIEF IN AMERICAN EXCEPTIONALISM

A nation that is great does not need to boast about it! It will be known without promotion. Other nations don't appreciate hearing, by implication, that their country offers much less than the U.S. does. The citizens of many countries actually prefer their own country's ways and culture to U.S. culture. Many Europeans, especially the French, feel their lives are more satisfying. They only work 35 hours a week, have six weeks of vacation, eat better food at a slower pace, and enjoy more cultural diversity by being European citizens.

America's best antidote to doting on exceptionalism is for U.S. citizens to focus on further improving the performance of capitalism and democracy in the U.S. There is much improvement needed. The American government needs stronger policies to reduce poverty in the U.S. Policies are also needed to create more jobs, fix our deteriorating infrastructure, reduce air and water pollution, and improve our education and health system. By doing these things, more Americans can be justly proud of their country.

4. GROWING PUBLIC ANTIPATHY TOWARD GOVERNMENT

Citizens in many countries view their government with despair. Their government takes a big chunk of their hard-earned income in income taxes, sales taxes, and licensing fees. Many citizens experience a huge bureaucracy whose service is bad, where there are long delays, and where there is no recourse to alternative suppliers. Governments pass a lot of regulations that limit business freedom and raise business costs. Consider the money that businesses have to pay to reduce pollution, to make food safer, and to renew licenses. Add to this the many deep anti-government critiques that criticize government at every opportunity. The average U.S. citizen will hear much more excoriation of government than praise, leaving many citizens with the feeling that government is too big, too wasteful, and inefficient.

On these occasions, citizens need to be reminded about the good things that come from their taxes. They get better roads and highways, safer cars, competent police and firefighters, a free public education system, public parks, and an adequately prepared military establishment. Citizens in some other countries see their government in a positive light. The French are proud of the role that their government played in developing the beauty of Paris streets and vistas. Citizens in Japan and South Korea give their governments high marks for caring about the people. Years ago, the Harvard economist John Kenneth Galbraith complained that the government does too little rather than too much. He agreed that Americans benefitted greatly from the work of the private sector but he saw a poverty of public goods. A middle class American may drive his expensive car to work but average only ten miles an hour because of traffic congestion; or drive his family to a public park only to find it ravaged by garbage, vermin, and homeless people looking for food. He titled his book *The Affluent Society* with tongue-in-cheek because so much of the affluent society was not affluent.

How can more Americans be moved to take a more balanced view of their government and the country's accomplishments? Here are some initiatives:

- Teach public school children more about the good things that government does and can do. Students in a civics class can play the role of a mayor, governor, president or a legislator facing a set of alternative decisions involving spending more public money to improve citizens' lives and consider what choices they would make. We need to bring together people criticizing and praising government and debate their opinions. We need columnists who invite people to submit their good and bad experiences with government.
- Governments at all levels must become more businesslike and transparent in their operations and decisions. Periodically, they need to give a public accounting of what the government accomplished with their tax money. As government performs better, there will be less criticism of government.
- Respected institutions should search for examples of good government behavior, present awards, and circulate these awards broadly as examples of good government.

5. TWO-PARTY GRIDLOCK PREVENTING NEEDED LEGISLATION

A political party represents a set of core beliefs. Members are expected to accept these beliefs and use them in the voting process.

The Republican Party believes in 'freedom', 'personal responsibility', and 'private enterprise' as absolutes. The Democratic Party believes in 'caring for others' and an 'active government to correct problems.' Obviously these two belief systems conflict and this explains why the two-party gridlock situation persists.

Consider the issue of whether abortions should be banned. Our current law says that a woman has the right to choose an abortion up to 24 or 28 weeks. Yet many Republicans would like to change the law and ban abortions. Until this happens, they do everything to make it more difficult for women to have an abortion. They try to cut down the number of family planning clinics. They want to require a woman to see what her baby in her womb looks like at the time of the planned abortion. They would like her to delay her decision and listen to messages against abortions. Granted that there is a legitimate debate about late-term abortions of fully formed babies, but many Republicans want to ban all abortions even if the woman was raped or the baby will be a seriously defective child.

The Republicans, in wanting to ban abortions, are technically straying from their core belief in freedom. Shouldn't it be for the woman to have the choice? Isn't the Republican position on abortion a contradiction? Here is how the Republicans rationalize their interference with the woman's freedom. They postulate that a new 'person' exists from the moment of conception. That person has a right to live. That person would choose the freedom to live. Abortion is therefore murder. By banning abortions, both mother and child will both live. This is a greater good than letting one person live and the other person be murdered.

The Democrats counter that the egg–sperm combination is only a chemical mix at conception and not a person. The chemical mix has the potential of becoming a person after it is formed more physically. Democrats see the woman as facing a difficult decision. She may be a pregnant teenager who is only 14, unmarried, living in poverty, and with her single mother who is ill. The girl doesn't want to bring a baby into the world who will end up living in poverty like herself and who would end her own chances of finishing school, getting a career, and improving her life. How can we say that this teenager is irrational in deciding to have an abortion? How can believers in freedom deny this girl her own? Aren't they bringing in a religious view and forgetting that the nation believes in the separation of church and state?

The same issue arises with guns. Virtually all Republicans vote solidly in favor of the freedom to buy and have a gun. Some Republicans want to use a gun recreationally, or have the gun for personal protection. But Democrats want to limit the number and kinds of guns that a person has. They don't want past criminals and mentally unstable people to buy a gun. They don't want people to carry their guns into schools, churches, or public gatherings. What is the belief of Democrats? Many Democrats believe that more guns will increase the chances that more innocent people will be hurt.

The deep Republican belief in freedom is also tested in the case of businesses that want to produce a product that might be harmful. Republicans favored the right of companies to make, sell, and glamorize cigarettes against the evidence that smokers will increase their chance of dying early from lung disease, cancer, or a heart attack. Democrats argue that cigarette smoking also creates secondary harm to others in the vicinity of smokers. They argue that cigarette smoking should be discouraged and confined to only certain locations. They leave the smoker with the freedom to smoke. They do not favor a total ban on smoking. Anti-smokers simply want the freedom to mount public campaigns to discourage young people from starting to smoke and to make everyone aware of the harm that smoking can cause.

What can be done to reduce the clash of these two belief systems? Each party has some members who are less absolute about their belief system. One often hears a Republican say that he is conservative on economic matters and liberal on social matters. An effort should be made by more 'liberal' Republicans to get together and support each other. An effort should be made by more 'conservative' Democrats to get together and support each other. The final step would be for both groups to meet each other and exhibit an air of openness and interest in each other's ideas.

6. THE GROWING ROLE OF MONEY IN POLITICS

Getting elected takes lots of money. In earlier times, many candidates spent their own money or raised money from their immediate family, friends, and acquaintances. They used the money to pay for their transportation from city to city, to pay for lodging, entertainment, rallies, teas, newspaper ads, and the like. They needed to hire staff members to make these arrangements, to find out where to speak next, and to create and distribute publicity. Even if a particular candidate won the election, the pay from their new position in the legislature would not cover the cost they spent getting elected. The candidate is okay because most of the cost was born by donors. Or the candidate was rich enough so it didn't matter. Many voters prefer wealthy candidates because they would be less dependent on donors. Wealthy candidates aren't in politics for the money. But the cost did matter to candidates who didn't have enough money to pay their bills. A newly elected legislator would face many temptations to go after new money by favoring their donors' interests.

Getting elected today is costlier than ever. The candidate must build a movement not only with volunteers but with squads of specialists—pollsters, market researchers, political strategists, data analysts, advertising experts, and public relations experts. The candidate must choose these specialists carefully, knowing that the more he or she will pay, the better the specialists. Successful political campaigning requires elaborate election-building machinery. And given that in a contest of two, three or four candidates only one wins, one can appreciate how much money is burned up in the attempt to get a new politician elected.

Today's candidates depend on deep-pocketed donors. A presidential candidate needs a billionaire or two to back him. Money will also come from lobbyists and companies who see the candidate as someone who can help vote in their interests. We all know politicians who always favor gun rights or the interests of the oil or pharmaceutical industries.

There is no easy answer as to how to reduce the amount of money going into politics. Among the proposals are:

- Create a shorter political advertising period in terms of when political advertising can start. Great Britain limits advertising campaigning to 30 days before the election voting day. The argument is that any candidate can get out his or her message within 30 days. All candidates would benefit by not needing as much money, and hopefully all of them would agree to this rule. However, it doesn't limit their public speaking activities and rallies.
- Regulate lobbying activities more effectively. The public needs to know who the lobbyists are and to whom they gave their money. Make sure that ex-Congress people cannot sign up with a lobbyist firm for three years after leaving Congress. Lawrence Lessig has written extensively on how to limit lobbying and election spending.

7. GERRYMANDERING EMPOWERING INCUMBENTS TO GET RE-ELECTED FOREVER

Both political parties engage in gerrymandering when they are in power. To improve the chance of their candidate's re-election, they draw up better redistricting lines that leave more of their voters in the Congress member's district. This may lead to some strange shapes of voting districts. Republican candidates get a better chance of getting re-elected if their districts contain more suburbs, while Democratic candidates benefit by including more of a major city in their district.

State legislatures will get away with gerrymandering unless the minority party actively intervenes by pointing out which voting districts of opponents have been grossly gerrymandered. They call for the legislature to appoint an independent redistricting commission to study the changes and modify them. This has led a number of states to redraw voting district boundaries.

8. CAUCUSES AND PRIMARIES LEADING CANDIDATES TO ADOPT MORE EXTREME POSITIONS

A number of candidates will typically compete in a party's caucuses or primary to be the party's standard bearer. In a closed primary, only party members will be allowed to vote. Typically, the more activist members will show up to vote. For example, many of the Republican Party's Tea Party members are likely to show up to vote for their favorite candidate. This leads candidates to show that that they are in accord with Tea Party issues. Around the country, many Republican candidates will emerge who embrace the Tea Party's positions on issues. The Democratic Party also has its splintered and activist groups.

The fact that activist groups vote heavily in primaries can result in both parties presenting standard bearers who are less representative of the average party voter preference. The leading candidates of the two parties can be more extreme from each other and therefore less likely to compromise on proposed legislation. This goes a long way to explaining the persistence and increase in the level of political gridlock.

The basic solution is to get more typical party members to show up and vote during primary elections. But primary elections are poorly attended historically. Maybe only one-third of the party members show up to vote. The party needs to campaign to its members that they have an obligation to vote, otherwise they won't get the candidate they want. Party members should feel obligated to get other party members to vote.

The other option is to run open primaries. This allow independents to vote as well as members of the other party. The latter may cast their votes for the poorest candidates in order that their own candidate would have a better chance against the other party's candidate.

9. CONTINUOUS CONFLICT BETWEEN THE PRESIDENT AND CONGRESS

Every new President starts out wanting to work well with Congress. This is in his or her interest. If the President alienates members of Congress from the start, they won't support the President's legislative initiatives. The President could gain their goodwill by being legislatively less active. This means that the President won't push for much change, letting Congress determine what has to be changed. But if the President makes this choice, he or she will not end the presidency with much of a leadership record.

To be legislatively inactive is a high price to pay for a new President who has stumped hard for certain issues and improvements. Barack Obama clearly had a vision of strong changes needed in healthcare, clean energy, reducing our military involvements, and so on. Clearly, he was going to come into conflict with more Congress members of the other party, and he would need greater support from his own party. But even his own party split with him on some issues, such as trying to pass the nuclear deal with Iran. So the stronger that a President asserts leadership, the greater his conflict with Congress.

If Congress in addition is undergoing a high level of political gridlock, the new President will not be able to pass much needed legislation. The public will be disappointed in their new President and disappointed with Congress as well. It will take a new President with considerable human relations skills and who is privy to very private information about leading Congress members to be able to overcome their resistance and get some bills passed. Lyndon Johnson was such a President who knew enough about all the members of Congress to make it worthwhile for them to support some of his measures.

The most likely effective President is one who gets elected with a strong victory of his party in both the House and in the Senate. It also helps if this President has a good sense of humor. This happened when Ronald Reagan became the 40th U.S. President. Bill Clinton, the 42nd President, also became more effective by making concessions to the Republican Party so that he became more centrist and could work more effectively with the Republican Party.

So the formula for a President to be successful with Congress includes the following:

- Move to a more centrist position rather than be on the far Left or the far Right.
- Give concessions to the other party in exchange for support for his or her issues.
- Have a sense of humor and openness with Congress and the public.
- Get to know individual Congress members deeply in terms of their weaknesses and strengths and spend a lot of time with them.

10. CONTINUOUS CONFLICT BETWEEN THE FEDERAL AND STATE GOVERNMENTS

Some public activities and issues are best settled locally or state-wide and others are best settled nationally. K–12 education (pre-college grading system used in the U.S. and Canada) has traditionally been designed and financed locally on the grounds that people are at different educational levels from place to place and each voting district has to decide on how much education they think is needed, on the best way to deliver it, and on how much money to spend delivering it. The Department of Education in the federal government does not run local educations but aspires to assist in setting higher standards. The Common Core curriculum program and the 'No Child Left Behind' Act are efforts at the federal level to raise educational standards, but it is clear that many cities and states resent these programs that invade their control of local education.

States and cities also want the right to set up their own laws on the purchase and use of guns. Federal authorities have set up some commonsense rules that guns don't get into the hands of mentally unstable persons or criminals. Still Congress has prevented the federal government to standardize these gun controls sufficiently. Normally we would want the law to limit the number of guns that a person can own and the types of guns that they could own.

With other issues, a stronger case can be made for standardizing the law and making it apply to all cities and states. Marriage law should be defined nationally, not locally. Done locally, a city might bar marriage between a white and black couple and between members of the same sex. Today virtually all states require persons to be 18 years of age or older if they want to get married—with the two exceptions of Nebraska (19) and Mississippi (21). Some states allow female minors below 18 to marry without parental or judicial consent if she is pregnant. But it took a new federal law to allow same-sex marriage. Without it, couples married legally in one state would not have their marriage recognized as legal in another state.

It is very important to standardize rules and regulations on a national basis when it comes to commerce. The Interstate Commerce Act was passed to harmonize trade practices among the states. Producers of branded products, such as Procter & Gamble, Kraft, and others, don't want to look up the regulations for every city and state when they sell their brands nationally. They expect a high degree of commercial standardization across states. Still there are some businesses, such as those producing alcoholic beverages and pharmaceutical products, that have to understand different laws regulating their products in each city or state.

Many people prefer keeping control in the hands of local people who know more about their own capabilities, requirements and public attitudes. The U.S. was founded by a group of early Americans who didn't want to pay a tax on tea and received no benefit for it. Local autonomy is a deep instinct in the American mindset, and Congress members are always ready to argue for local and state control because they have to answer back to their voters.

At the same time, when differences become so pronounced between different regions in their educational levels, health facilities, and gun laws, there are many people who would press for more standardization to equalize opportunities and abilities. The net result is that there will continue to be continuous contention between states' rights and federal standardization.

11. THE SUPREME COURT'S READINESS TO REVISE LEGISLATIVE ACTIONS

Americans have a deep belief that laws should be made by Congress and not tampered with by the President or the Supreme Court. The view is that Congress carries out the will of the people. Yet in the famous 1803 case of *Marbury v. Madison*, the Supreme Court voted unanimously that the Court could declare an act of Congress unconstitutional even though the Constitution did not give the Supreme Court the power to do so. This would be greatly objectionable if most Supreme Court decisions were fairly unanimous that a law is unconstitutional. That would mean nine justices changed a law that 500 members of Congress decided to pass. But so many cases handled by these nine justices result in a 5-to-4 decision. This means that nine justices are making or canceling a law passed by Congress in the public interest.

Look at the outrage of Senator Ted Cruz when the same-sex marriage law was passed because so many people want traditional marriage to rule. Look at the battle over abortion where many states want to pass their own laws on abortion. In *Roe v. Wade* (1973), the U.S. Supreme Court, in a 7-to-2 vote, stated that abortion bans were unconstitutional in every state, legalizing abortion throughout the U.S.

Because many Supreme Court decisions are decided by a 5-to-4 majority, this tends to reduce confidence in the Court's decisions. Citizens think that the justices are voting ideologically rather than on the unique facts in each case. Ideally, new justices should be ideologically neutral where in each case one couldn't predict what any justice would vote. Justice Kennedy is an example in that he normally votes more conservatively but in a few cases he votes more liberally. This could not be said of Justice Thomas; his vote is wholly predictable. As Congress becomes more ready to look for future justices who are less ideological, court decisions will find greater acceptance. Unfortunately, the President will always recommend a justice for consideration who thinks like his party thinks, and the opposition party will oppose that person if they suspect that he or she will move too much with the other party.

12. THE DIFFICULTY OF PASSING NEW AMENDMENTS

Since the passage of the U.S. Constitution in September 17, 1787, approximately 11,539 proposals to amend the Constitution have been introduced. This number should not come as a surprise. With all the changes that have taken place in our economics, international relations, technology, and society, one would have expected more amendments to have passed. Since the adoption of the Bill of Rights—the first ten Amendments to the Constitution, ratified in 1791—only 17 Amendments have cleared the hurdles to be codified in the nation's founding document. The last Amendment, number 27, was ratified in 1992.

There are different ways to amend the Constitution, but only two have been used:

• The most common method has led to the passage of 26 out of the 27 Amendments. Both the House and Senate vote on the proposed amendment and each must pass it with a two-thirds majority. If this happens, the amendment is sent to state legis-latures for their approval. Here a majority in three-quarters of all state legislatures must vote to approve the proposed amendment. This means that only 13 states can block a proposed amendment from being ratified.

- The Convention of States method allows for the legislatures of two-thirds of the states to call for a national convention to amend the Constitution. These amend-ments would have to be approved by three-quarters of state conventions that are called to consider these amendments. This amendment method has never been used.

- The 21st Amendment, repealing the 18th Amendment prohibiting the selling of alcohol, was passed in a different way. Two-thirds of both houses of Congress voted to send this amendment to the states for ratification, but instead of insisting that three-quarters of state legislatures approve the amendment, Congress specified that 'this article shall be inoperative unless it shall have been ratified as an amendment to the Constitution by conventions in the several States [...] within seven years.' Congress did so because proponents believed elected delegates to these conventions were more likely to reflect public opinion on Prohibition. Within ten months of Congress' passage, the 21st Amendment was approved.

- Passage of the 27th Amendment, which was ratified in 1992, took by far the longest period of time between proposal and ratification! It was first proposed by James Madison in 1789 to prevent Congress from voting to alter their pay during a con-gressional session. It had been approved by a half-dozen states but then laid dormant. Americans' frustrations with congressional pay raises grew in the late 20th century and gained steam, until the 27th Amendments was finally ratified in 1992.

It is clear that amending the Constitution takes an overwhelming agreement that some situation badly needs correction. Given how many amendment proposals have been made and how few have passed gives credit to the founding fathers about their perspicacity in setting up our Constitution. Our Constitution has not become irrelevant. At the same time, it is only the liberal interpretations of some distin-guished justices in the past that brought us to view the Constitution as a living document rather than a frozen document that ignores all the changes that have occurred in society. One doesn't need many amendments when the Supreme Court acts wisely to adapt the Constitution to the new world in which we are living.[1]

13. THE DIFFICULTY OF DEVELOPING A SOUND FOREIGN POLICY

The making of a sound American foreign policy involves a number of players and an endless number of influencers. Foreign policy initiatives can come from the President, the State Department, or Congress. The President retains com-mand of the military and the ability to make appointments and handle treaties. The President is also the person who receives foreign representatives and works with them to achieve accord.

The best arrangement is where the President works cordially with Congress on all major foreign policy initiatives. Here is where the trouble starts. Congressional members come from two parties who have quite different views on what U.S. foreign policy should be overall and what it should be toward particular countries such as China, Russia, North Korea, Iran, Iraq, and other key nations. The President largely represents the views of the party that got him or her elected. The President must rely on supplying facts and arguments to members of the other party to justify positions taken on any major foreign policy initiative. Compromises are inevitable. The President works fast and closely to changing events in the world where Congress moves slowly to debate or approve presidential initiatives. The President is often prevented from satisfying foreign power's requests or actions in a reasonable time.

Many trade agreements and military initiatives must wait for the approval of Congress. Congress can take their own foreign policy initiatives through resolutions and policy statements, legislative directives, legislative pressure, informal advice, or funding denials. The executive branch can support or try to change congressional policies as it sees its interest and the public's interest.

It is difficult to say who is to be credited with any aspect of our foreign policy because it evolves out of the shared work of both branches of government. Foreign policy does not take the form of a grand design but rather is the result of individual policies occurring in or with different countries and regions. At times the President plays the role of a strong leader in foreign policy and at other times Congress dominates the foreign policy agenda.

14. MAKING GOVERNMENT AGENCIES MORE ACCOUNTABLE

The public has a right to expect government agencies to have a real and valid purpose and to be run efficiently. Each government agency should be established to meet a real public need that cannot be met by the private sector. The agency should be adequately funded to achieve its objectives. Its work should be reviewed periodically to determine whether it should be terminated, expanded, or stay as it is.

Every agency can expect to receive criticism from those who are regulated and from those who feel that the service is lacking. Many complain that there are too many U.S. government agencies, many have overlapping or competing responsibilities, many cost the taxpayers too much money, and many are bureaucratic and slow in making decisions. Business groups in particular think that these agencies cost them delays and require them to drop a planned strategy or require them to increase their costs, all adding up to discouraging investment and slowing down the growth of the economy.

Yet the public wants competent and capable agencies to make sure that food and drugs are acceptable (Federal Drug Administration); climate is relatively free of pollution (Environment Protection Agency); products are safe (Consumer Product Safety Commission); airlines and airports are safe (Federal Aviation Administration); equal employment opportunities exist (Equal Employment Opportunity Commission); and that the stock market is run fairly (Securities and Exchange Commission).

The main need is to run a good civil service operation that recruits qualified employees and managers, and pays them adequately to administer efficiently the business of government.

CONCLUSION

Every democracy has its warts. America permitted the ownership of slaves until Lincoln's Emancipation Proclamation in 1863. It also deprived women of the right to vote until 1920 with the passage of the 16th Amendment. More recently, the U.S. has been moving from a 'government by the people and for the people' to a 'government by the 1% and for the 1%.' This chapter has reviewed 14 of the current warts and suggests possible reforms. No governing system can or should remain the same. The system must be resilient and adapt to new forces. The issue is whether citizens have the will to improve democracy or allow it to drift away from its original values and principles.

The columnist Thomas Friedman sees the greatest sources of strength to be 'a culture of entrepreneurship', 'an ethic of pluralism', and the 'quality of govern-ing institutions.' He sees all of these falling behind. The Harvard scholar Samuel Huntington sees the democratic creed to consist of three core values: egalitari-anism, liberty, and individualism. Most citizens would not want these core values to wither under the strong forces of technology, globalization, and income inequality. Citizens in a democracy must feel that their political system provides them with an equal voice, free expression, personal safety, and the rule of law. Let's hope that all these values will be protected and preserved.

NOTE

1   http://classroom.synonym.com/four-ways-pass-amendment-constitution-11631. html (accessed 03.03.16).

CHAPTER 11

DEALING WITH THE MAJOR UNRESOLVED GOVERNMENT POLICY ISSUES

'Problems can become opportunities when the right people come together.'
Robert Redford

The American people and their representatives must decide on a great number of issues each year. Many of the most important issues continue year after year without any resolution. Congress seems to prefer to 'kick the can down the road' rather than collaborate on real policy solutions.

I have chosen to comment on 16 of the most persistent policy issues. They are, in alphabetical order:

1 Abortion
2 Campaign finance
3 Climate and pollution
4 Consumer protection
5 Drug wars
6 Gun control
7 Healthcare
8 Immigration
9 Incarceration and prisons
10 Infrastructure
11 Military and defense
12 National debt
13 Poverty
14 Social Security and retirement
15 Student loans
16 Taxes

Let's now take a brief look at each one.

1. ABORTION

Roe v. Wade, 410 U.S. 113 (1973), is a landmark decision by the U.S. Supreme Court on the issue of abortion. Decided simultaneously with a companion case, *Doe v. Bolton*, the Court ruled 7-to-2 that a right to privacy under the due process clause of the 14th Amendment extended to a woman's decision to have an abortion, but that this right must be balanced against the state's two legitimate interests in regulating abortions: protecting women's health and protecting the potentiality of human life. Arguing that these state interests became stronger over the course of a pregnancy, the Court resolved this balancing test by tying state regulation of abortion to the third trimester of pregnancy. Once the newborn could potentially live outside the mother's womb, this decision might no longer be allowed. 'Viability' is usually placed at about 7 months (28 weeks) but could occur earlier, even at 24 weeks.[1]

Over time, those who despised this decision attempted to weaken it by legal and other means. They called themselves 'pro-life' as opposed to the supporters of this decision who were for 'pro-choice.' The pro-life group argued that a human being begins at the point of conception and aborting that human being is tantamount to murder. They said that the fetus has civil rights as well as the mother. The extreme members of the pro-life group say that an abortion should not be allowed in the case of rape or even when the unborn child is likely to be born defectively as indicated by a medical preview early in the pregnancy. This group has taken to vigorous grassroots demonstrations near planned parenthood clinics, in a few cases even killing a physician who has conducted abortions.

Pro-life supporters have taken legal steps to get state legislatures to put more difficulties in the path of a woman's right to choose abortion. Texas has ruled that clinics need medical equipment and procedures up to the standards of modern hospitals. Some planned parenthood centers have had to close their doors because they could not afford that level of equipment. Other states want a woman to submit to seeing the unborn fetus in her womb before she makes a decision. Some states require a young woman to get her parents' agreement or to go through a waiting period.

The pro-choice group argue that women face a very difficult decision that they are not happy to make but that they have weighed the pros and cons and decided abortion is the best solution. Thus a pregnant teenager might have to give up the idea of going to college and take care of a baby without a husband or good job prospects. Each woman should be free to do what she sees as being in her best interest. The pro-choice group does not believe that a human being exists at the time of conception and does not believe that the particular beliefs of a religious movement are relevant to this scientific question of whether a human being exists at the moment of fertilization.

The prospects of finding a compromise on this issue are very low. The law remains on the side of the mother's freedom to choose. At the same time, the pro-life group continues to try to stop or delay abortions to the extent possible.

2. CAMPAIGN FINANCE

Political election campaigns used to be simple: Get a lot of citizens to sign a petition backing you as a candidate; get your political party to endorse you as one of the candidates; start talking to different groups about your beliefs and experience; smile, shake hands, kiss babies, and you might win the nomination.

Today the first thing is to find some rich folks who believe in you. You will need a lot of money. If you can score with a billionaire, you are off to a good start. But don't neglect ordinary Joes and be sure to collect their $5 as well.

Here are the current rules for donor gifts to campaigns and candidates:

* A donor can give as much as $2,700 per candidate in that election cycle.
* A donor can give as much as $5,000 to a PAC per election cycle.
* A donor can give as much as $33,400 to a political party per year.
* A donor (individual or corporation) can give an unlimited amount to a Super PAC that election cycle but the donor's name will be public.
* A donor (individual or corporation) can give an unlimited amount to a social welfare organization and their name can remain private.

The Supreme Court's 5-to-4 decision in favor of *Citizens United* means that every company and organization is free to give money to PACs and Super PACs. A PAC exists to support a particular candidate and must publicly list the donors and amounts. The Supreme Court's 2010 *Citizens United* decision led to the setup of Super PACs. Technically, Super PACs must be 'operated exclusively to promote social welfare.' Political activity is allowed but must not be the organization's 'primary' mission. Yet the current IRS commissioner said that groups could spend up to 49% of revenues on political activity and still keep their tax exemption.

Clearly, rich donors and corporations have many ways to give lots of money to candidates and parties of their choice. Many proposals have been advanced for limiting the amount of political campaign expenditures:

- Require all candidates to apply for public funds to finance their campaign. All candidates would receive the same amount to spend as they wish. They would also agree not to accept additional money from individual donors, corporations, unions, or nonprofit organizations. The election period would be confined to 30 days of electioneering as in the U.K.
- Keep the present arrangement but require Super PACs to list the names and amounts from donors and strictly limit the percentage that can go to supporting a candidate as opposed to promoting a social issue.
- Terminate the *Citizens United* decision which said that companies are people who are free to promote candidates. Severely limit the amount of funds that all organizations can give to support a political candidate.

3. CLIMATE AND POLLUTION

According to the World Health Organization (WHO), 223,000 people died in 2010 from lung cancer caused by exposure to air pollution. Many of the cities in China and East Asia are polluted. European cities such as Sofia (Bulgaria) and Krakow (Poland) are highly polluted as well as U.S. cities such as Bakersfield and Fresno, California. U.S. and Western European cities are relatively less polluted than Asian cities because of tighter anti-pollution investments required from companies.

Water pollution is a growing problem as well. Our oceans have been a dumping ground for harmful chemicals and refuse that have been poisoning fish and sea life. Currently micro-beads used in preparing cosmetics are populating our waters, causing more fish to die.

The U.S. established the Environmental Protection Agency (EPA) in 1970 under President Nixon to protect human health and the environment. The EPA established fair practices for sharing the cost and responsibility of producing pollution. One policy is to set a limit on the amount of permissible carbon pollution and require companies to use cap and trade. Currently some politicians are impugning the leadership of the EPA as putting too much of a regulation burden on industry.

The ultimate question is how much curbing of pollution is desirable given that it will slow down the rate of economic growth. The columnist George Will denies climate change as scientifically established and complains about how many jobs and economic growth are being lost due to regulatory measures to reduce pollution.

Can Congress develop a clearer estimate of how many jobs are lost with different levels of effort to reduce air and water pollution?

4. CONSUMER PROTECTION

Capitalism has been a driving force in raising the living standards of people around the world. Companies are free to design and sell products and services to whoever might be interested in buying them. Companies set up sales goals and train and motivate their marketers to sell as many units as possible. Marketers are rewarded according to how much they sell. Sales people might try to convince a family to buy a home or car that they cannot really afford. They offer easy finance so that the monthly payments seem small and feasible even though they might carry a high hidden financing charge.

In this context, we can cite a number of reasons why consumers might require some protection:

- Credit card firms, banks, and retailers might make it too easy for consumers to buy things that they cannot afford.
- Some sellers might make or sell products that can hurt consumers. Tobacco companies make products that injure the health of smokers. Food companies or restaurants might sell food that is out of date or harmful to people's health. Manufacturers might make products such as ladders or cars that carry a defect that might harm the user or others.
- Some sellers might sell perfectly safe products but exaggerate their performance. Consider a pharmaceutical company claiming that its pill will bring relief when it is only a placebo. Marketers are storytellers and might claim much more product performance or benefits than will be delivered.

For these and other reasons, countries establish and fund laws and a consumer protection bureau that tests products, makes sure of their safety, and makes sure that the sellers' claims are supportable.

5. DRUG WARS

President Nixon declared a 'war on drugs' in June 1971 and he increased the size of federal drug control agencies. He pushed through measures including mandatory sentencing. The drugs included marijuana, opium, cocaine, heroin, and psychedelics.

Regarding marijuana, in 1972 a commission recommended decriminalizing the possession and distribution of marijuana for personal use, but Nixon rejected this. Yet between 1973 and 1977, 11 states decriminalized marijuana possession. In October 1977, the Senate Judiciary Committee decriminalized possession of up to one ounce of marijuana for personal use.

In the 1980s, parents began to complain about the high rates of teen marijuana use. President Reagan started a highly-publicized anti-drug campaign with the slogan 'Just Say No' and pushed for zero tolerance policies. This led to skyrocketing rates of incarceration increasing the number of people in prison from 473,368 in 1980 to over 2,042,479 in 2001.

Bill Clinton, during his 1992 presidential campaign, advocated treatment instead of incarceration but after winning the presidency his administration continued to escalate the drug war. Only toward the end of his presidency did he call for a re-examination of the policy of imprisonment and preferred to see marijuana decriminalized.

President George W. Bush allocated even more money to fight the drug wars, including launching 40,000 paramilitary-style SWAT raids on Americans every year.

Yet efforts at reforming the drug laws continued. Many notable figures— Michael Bloomberg, Barack Obama—publicly admitted to using marijuana in their youth. The mood is changing now, especially in view of 2,220,300 adult inmates in 2013. States such as Colorado and Oregon are currently engaged in liberalizing the use of marijuana, especially for medical use, but moving toward recreational uses.

What should America's hard drug policy be? There are six possible policies:

1   Keep spending on the 'War Against Drugs' and imprison drug sellers and keep a zero intolerance for drug users with continued stiff prison sentences.
2   Keep spending on the 'War Against Drugs' but lighten the sentence for personal marijuana use, let judges have discretion to go below the normal sentence level, and put more money into treatment than incarceration.
3   Give more inmates the chance to earn early release by participating in educational and other rehabilitative programming; seal or expunge juvenile records so that people are not burdened for life because of crimes they committed when they were young; and make it easier for older inmates to seek early release.
4   Make personal hard drug use a personal matter: Imprison drug sellers only.
5   Make personal hard drug use a personal matter: Open state-owned and operated stores to sell marijuana and other drugs to keep them safe and earn revenue.
6   Make personal hard drug use a personal matter: Let private enterprise manage the sale of marijuana.

Progress is inevitably slow but there is new momentum behind drug policy reform right now. We look forward to a future where hard drug policies are guided by scientific research and effective promotion is used to convince young people and others to say no to drugs.

6. GUN CONTROL

The U.S. is the most gun-toting nation in the world. In many states, people can buy a gun without much background check regarding mental stability or criminality. They can buy as many guns as they want. They can carry their guns into shopping centers, schools, and churches.

This love for guns goes back into American history. Movies dramatize the role of guns in the lawless West and in the hands of famous gangsters such as John Dillinger and Al Capone. The right to own guns is an interpretation of the 2nd Amendment to the U.S. Constitution which states that 'a well-regulated militia, being necessary to the security of a free state, the right of the people to keep and bear arms, shall not be infringed.' Technically, this was a right for militias but not for individuals. The Supreme Court failed to go back to the Constitution's intent.

Many people get killed by guns—including gang wars and gangster wars, love quarrels, and children playing with a gun, and an occasional madman who shoots down several people before being captured or killed. Every incident gets the public stirred to press Congress for legislation to curb gun ownership. President Obama has spoken out in these dark moments, some would say correctly while some would say inappropriately during times of mourning, to make the case for stricter gun laws.

However, the powerful National Rifle Association (NRA) and hunting associations constantly lobby the members of Congress not to pass any legislation restricting the right to own guns. The NRA makes it clear that any Congress member who supports curbing guns will not get any financial support from the NRA and even will suffer from advertising against his or her re-election. The NRA is considered the most powerful lobby group in Washington.

What could be done about gun ownership? Here are some options:

- Do nothing and allow the status quo to continue. Concede that not much can be changed. Accept arguments that murderers are the problem rather than their weapons.
- Pass a law that requires gun ownership information from every individual on the specific guns owned.

- Limit the number of guns owned to two and prohibit guns that can be loaded with more than six bullets.
- Ban guns from being carried in public. Their use is limited to homes and hunting grounds.

7. HEALTHCARE

The U.S. has established four health insurance programs: Medicare, Medicaid, the Children's Health Insurance Program (CHIP), and the Affordable Care Act. These insurance programs account for 24% of the federal budget in 2014, or $836 billion. About $511 billion went to Medicare to provide health coverage to around 54 million people over the age of 65 or who have disabilities. Medicaid and CHIP made up the remainder to provide health care or long-term care to about 70 million low-income children, parents, elderly people, and people with disabilities. Medicaid and CHIP require matching payments from the states.

On March 23, 2010, President Obama signed into law the Affordable Care Act (ACA) which introduced many new benefits, rights, and protections with the aim of ensuring that more U.S. citizens have access to affordable, quality healthcare. All persons are entitled to buy health insurance whatever their condition. ACA has as one of its purposes to decrease the rate of growth of healthcare spending and include other reforms.

Before ACA, an estimated 45 million Americans were without any insurance coverage. Either insurance companies refused to cover them or many Americans did not have the money to buy the insurance at its stated level of cost. This was viewed as a national disgrace. Many previous bills had been passed to remedy this situation but were unsuccessful until the State of Massachusetts under Governor Mitt Romney introduced a health care reform bill that became the model for the ACA.

ACA requires everyone to pay for healthcare insurance and choose the plan of their liking. This was required in order to raise the money needed to finance the new Act. Young people would have to buy health insurance. They could oppose this on the grounds that they are healthy and would prefer to buy health insurance when they are much older. The plan provided that those who were poor and who could not pay for insurance would be subsidized.

Ever since the plan was enacted, a majority of Republican members of Congress have tried to repeal the ACA or vitiate it in some way. The plan to repeal it came to the Supreme Court on June 28, 2012 and the Court upheld the plan. The general consensus is that the ACA has improved the nation's health coverage and reduced the rate of cost growth in healthcare.

The Medicaid program, which was created in 1965 by adding Title XIX to the Social Security Act, was also controversial in that the states had to bear some of the cost. Under this Act, the federal government provides matching funds to states to enable them to provide medical assistance to low-income individuals and families with limited resources. All U.S. citizens and legal residents with income up to 133% of the poverty line, including adults without dependent children, would qualify for coverage in any state that participates in the Medicaid program. Each state currently has broad leeway to determine who is eligible for its implementation of the program but must meet certain standards. States cannot be compelled to meet plans that aim to expand the program. But these reluctant states will continue to receive previously established levels of Medicaid funding. Many critics worry that Medicaid will not be able to continue to meet its financial requirements. Some states would like to limit or eliminate Medicaid and let poor consumers use the emergency rooms of hospitals if they need treatment.

The following policy alternatives need to be distinguished:

- Eliminate the ACA and return to the previous system of voluntary healthcare. The leading Republican candidates are unanimous in calling for repeal of the healthcare reform law—Donald Trump has called it a 'catastrophe' and Jeb Bush labeled it a 'monstrosity.' Yet they have not proposed a better healthcare plan to replace ACA.
- Keep the ACA and encourage its further growth. It has insured many more families and individuals and has led to some lowering of health costs.
- Add modifications to the ACA to protect people from co-payments and deductibles that have been rising faster than their wages. Hillary Clinton proposed creating a new tax credit of up to $5,000 to help families pay high out-of-pocket medical costs and would require insurers to cover three visits to the doctor each year before people start paying to meet their deductible.
- Replace the ACA with a single government payer system that expands Medicare to cover every American and that will bring down the cost by eliminating the need and costs of private insurance companies. The system would work very much the way the Veterans Health Care administration handles the health of U.S. veterans. This is favored by presidential candidate Senator Bernie Sanders.
- Reduce the exorbitant prices for prescription drugs in the U.S. that manufacturers set with no reasonable justification. Authorize Medicare to negotiate with drug companies to drive down prices and allow Americans to import cheaper drugs from other countries. Cap a patient's out-of-pocket drug spending at $250 a month. Republican candidates believe private negotiations and competition among drug companies are working just fine to curb drug costs, however.

8. IMMIGRATION

Immigration policy is a continuous and contentious issue in the U.S. because there are so many people who want to come to the U.S. and apply for citizenship. There have been past waves of immigrants from European countries such as Ireland, Italy, Germany, Russia, and Ukraine, seeking to leave behind the hardships they experienced in their countries. Then Asians started to come—laborers from China, persons fleeing from Vietnam, people from the Indian sub-continent, and others. Many educated technicians have wanted to come, if not for citizenship but as temporary skilled workers for U.S. companies who need their services.

Today the major immigration issue is the inflow of illegal immigrants from Mexico and Central America. The question is what to do with the 11 million illegal immigrants. There are four alternative proposals:

- Find them and send them all back to their country of origin. (This is the position of Donald Trump and several other Republicans.)
- Send them back except for those who were born here. (The U.S. Constitution says that anyone born in the U.S. has a right to stay here and become a citizen.)
- Provide an amnesty system for those illegals who have been here for a long time and are able bodied and working. Provide a path of several stages to move toward becoming an American citizen.
- Do nothing but make sure that further immigrants cannot enter the U.S. illegally by building the strongest protective wall and security system.

The Republicans favor proposals 1, 2 and 4 and the Democrats favor proposal 3.

9. INCARCERATION AND PRISONS

The U.S. has more prison inmates than any other nation. In 2013, 2,220,300 adults (almost 1% of America's population) were incarcerated in U.S. federal and state prisons and county jails. In addition, 4,751,400 adults in 2013 were on probation or on parole. This means that 6,899,000 adults—about 1 in every 35 of the U.S. resident population—were under correctional supervision. Of these, 54,148 were juveniles in juvenile detention centers in 2013.

Much of the prisoner increase came about with the policies of President Ronald Reagan, who wanted his Republican Party to be hard on crime. New rules were set and judges began to give longer sentences. Most of the prisons worked on punishment rather than on rehabilitation. Many prisoners were pushers of hard drugs and small-time consumers of hard drugs, all incarcerated in an effort to fight the war on drugs. In the need for more prisons, the government invited private firms to finance and locate prisons in specific towns that became part of the local economy.

The embarrassingly high number of prisoners has led in recent times to lighter sentences and to a switch in emphasis from punishment to rehabilitation. Prisons are teaching useful subjects that might provide prisoners with skills for employment after they leave prison. More work is going into aiding prisoners during their release to find an apartment and a job and not fall back into the lifestyle that led to his or her arrest. There is even talk of monitoring the ex-offender's movements over time and location to make sure that he or she is not relapsing into the same criminal behavior.

10. INFRASTRUCTURE

A major economic factor in the performance of an economy is the condition of its infrastructure—roads, bridges, ports, railways, airports, schools. The U.S. had been blessed with great infrastructure that steadily brought down the cost of delivering goods. Consider how other countries—such as China or India—are handicapped by insufficient or terrible roads and infrastructure, a problem that China now is tackling and India is now turning to.

But the quality of U.S. infrastructure is no longer satisfactory. It has not been renewed with regular maintenance. Civil engineers have been giving many of America's infrastructure components ratings of C- to D-. Some bridges have collapsed and many roads are full of potholes.

The truth is that maintaining quality infrastructure is very expensive. Money has dried up federally and in many states and cities. There was a good opportunity during the 2008–2011 Great Recession to put the unemployed and able to work on infrastructure and some of this was done, but not enough.

My proposal is to create an Infrastructure Office to constantly assess where infrastructure needs to be fixed. Some money would need to be switched from defense to fix the issues with infrastructure. High-quality domestic infrastructure is needed for internal defense, besides being a means of job creation.

11. MILITARY AND DEFENSE

The U.S. has built the strongest military force in the world. It has military stationed around the world. It has built many allies with NATO (North Atlantic Treaty Organization), Japan, Israel, Saudi Arabia, and other countries. It has the largest stockpile of nuclear weapons. It is a major manufacturer of military equipment and weapons.

By undertaking to build such a strong military force, it bears a great cost but it frees many of its allies from needing to arm themselves. While we spend money on arms, our allies can use their money to build their economies, economies that compete with us. One question is whether the U.S. has been too generous to its allies.

The perennial question is how much of the federal budget needs to go into the military and defense. About 18% of the federal budget, or $615 billion, pays for defense and security-related international activities. The bulk of this money goes to the Department of Defense. The question always is whether to increase this amount or reduce it. Does the Navy need more ships? Not long ago, Congress was trying to give more money to the military than it wanted. Members of Congress have military manufacturing operations in their states and want to keep the jobs going. Is the military equipment getting old and are there enough new equipment innovations to require a higher budget? Or is it time to reduce this budget and release more money to spend on education, infrastructure, healthcare, and social needs?

The policy alternatives are:

- Substantially increase military and defense spending to let U.S. enemies know that America is not becoming weak but ready to fight ISIS and other enemies.
- Keep the military budget around 18% of the federal budget and move the money into the highest priority equipment and defense needs.
- Reduce the military budget and move more money into improving our education, infrastructure, health system, and social need programs.
- Reduce the military budget and move the money into reducing federal debt so that America doesn't have to pay so much interest to finance the debt.

12. NATIONAL DEBT

In 2007, U.S. national debt (leaving out state and local debt) stood at $8.971 trillion dollars and gross domestic product (GDP) stood at $14.570 trillion.

Therefore national debt amounted to 61% of GDP. This is not a dangerous level of national debt to GDP. By 2014, national debt grew to $17.794 trillion while GDP grew to $17.522 trillion, or 102% of GDP. Conservatives are now acutely worried about this level of debt because:

- the U.S. government has to borrow the money from here and abroad (especially from China in the past); and
- the U.S. has to pay annual interest on the national debt. In 2013, net interest payments on the debt totaled $222.75 billion, or 6.23% of all federal outlays. The government's average interest rate paid on the debt was 2.43%. Fortunately, this is a very low interest rate. But imagine if heavy inflation started to take place. Interest rates would rise and this would greatly increase the tax burden of America's national debt.

There are only two ways to reduce the debt. The first is to cut federal expenditures. The usual targets are social benefit programs and social security payments, even though the defense budget warrants some reduction. The second is to raise taxes, especially on the rich. This is opposed by conservatives on the grounds that the rich would invest less and work less and shrink our GDP further. Here, therefore, is a prime example of the terrible party gridlock in contemporary politics where neither side wants to give in even a little. Unfortunately, each year adds another deficit and national debt grows even more.

13. POVERTY

About 15% of Americans live in poverty, as defined by the government's measures of what it takes to feed, clothe, and shelter different size families. It is embarrassing for such a rich country to have so many poor people. The country handles this by running a large number of social benefit programs, including food stamps, negative earned income credits, and social assistance programs. The nation tries to develop as many income earning opportunities as possible but some people continue to either fail to find a job or decide to stop looking for a job.

We are used to thinking of poverty as a cultural problem with a vicious circle. Poor people have too many children, need social assistance, become dependent on this assistance, and lose the incentive to emerge out of poverty. We talk about the war on poverty but the U.S. really doesn't have a strong plan for reducing the current levels of poverty. Poverty is a drain on lives, leads to depression, homelessness, and crime, and affects politics and social order.

Two efforts are needed. The first is to create more jobs. If the private sector can't produce enough jobs, we must create jobs in the public sector. We have seen that infrastructure is suffering and many more jobs can be created to improve infrastructure.

The other effort is to raise the minimum wage. For years, the minimum wage in America stood at $7.45 an hour, which comes close to $15,000 a year if one worked 8 hours a day for all 52 weeks. Even then, an income of $15,000 is substantially below poverty for an individual and certainly for a family. Fortunately, many U.S. cities are now taking action to raise the minimum wage to $10 or as much as $15, depending on the cost of living in that location. But even $15 an hour barely gets the earner out of the poverty class even though it is a step in the right direction.

14. SOCIAL SECURITY AND RETIREMENT

The Social Security Act was passed in 1935 under President Roosevelt's effort to help people during the Great Depression and afterwards. It guarantees monthly payments to persons who retire at the age of 65. Job holders are required in the meantime to pay a Social Security tax on income earned up to $118,500. Social Security law has been amended several times.

In 2014, 24% of the federal government budget, or $851 billion, was paid for Social Security. Social Security provided monthly retirement benefits averaging $1,329 to 39 million retired workers in December 2014. Social Security also provided benefits to 2.3 million spouses and children of retired workers, 6.1 million surviving children and spouses of deceased workers, and 10.9 million disabled workers and their eligible dependents in December 2014.

Republicans have largely argued that the Social Security fund will run out of money in 20 to 40 years because of the increasing ratio of retirees to the number of workers. Republicans would like to eliminate Social Security and let individual workers determine where they want to put their savings for retirement. The argument is that workers could earn a higher return on their savings than by giving their money to the government. President George W. Bush led a major attempt to replace Social Security, but he didn't succeed.

Democrats want to continue Social Security and even enlarge its benefits. They propose enhancing the amount of revenue going into Social Security by two measures:

- Require all job holders to pay a Social Security tax on their whole income, not just the income up to $118,000. This would deliver more funds from wealthier job holders.
- Use a means test in paying out Social Security benefits by paying out less or nothing to those who have high retirement savings, even though they paid a lot of taxes toward Social Security.

This leaves the following policy alternatives:

- Leave Social Security the way it is now.
- Collect more funds for Social Security by setting the same tax on everyone's income with no limit.
- Apply a means test and limit Social Security payments to only those with low retirement funds.
- Replace Social Security where employees choose a private plan for where they want to save a regular share of their earnings for use after they retire.
- Raise the payment age for Social Security to begin at age 67 or 70 instead of 65 to reduce the rate at which Social Security pays out its funds.

15. STUDENT LOANS

Although the nation believes in sending as many students to college as possible, the rising cost of college acts as a major deterrent. A German student can attend college at no cost, but an American student will face an annual cost of anywhere from $20,000 to $60,000 depending on the college, not to mention the student's lost income while attending college.

To enable a high level of college attendance, it is essential to make college loans available either through banks, colleges, or both. Today outstanding college student loans amount to $1.2 trillion. The average college student is carrying a student loan debt of $30,000. Upon graduation, most students have to start paying down their debt, which reduces the chance that they can buy a car, home, furniture, and other big ticket items. This reduces the demand for these goods and consequently reduces the U.S. economy's growth rate.

A number of proposals have been made to reduce student loan debt:

- Get the government to pay universities for college education by shifting money from defense or other categories.
- Get the government and universities to increase the amount of scholarship aid based on need, rather than merit.

- Limit the annual student debt repayment amount to 10% or less of the person's annual income.
- Cap the interest rate that students have to pay on borrowed money for college.

16. TAXES

The issue of taxes is always on the minds of the government and citizens. In fact, the U.S. government came into existence because of a tax dispute. The British, through the East India Company, put a heavy duty on tea imports. Three tea carrying ships arrived in the Boston Harbor. On December 16, 1773, as many as 7,000 local citizens came to the docks, demanding that the ships leave the harbor without landing the tea or payment of any duty. The Collector of Customs refused. Early that evening, a group of about 200 men, some dressed as American Indians, descended on the three ships and dumped the tea cargoes into the harbor waters. This tea tax was the last straw for the American colonies, who would no longer allow the British government to impose taxes without Americans having a single representative in the British Parliament. The slogan became: 'No taxation without representation.' This and other grievances sparked the American Revolutionary War.

Taxes have to be raised separately by federal, state, and local governments. State and local governments need the taxes to pay for police and firefighters, schools, road construction, and other local services. They rely mainly on real estate taxes on residential and business property and sales taxes on consumer purchases. Most of the states also set an income tax for their residents.

The federal government has to charge a large number of taxes and fees to support its huge annual budget of $3.5 trillion (2014). Most of the budget goes toward:

- Defense and International Security Assistance: 18%
- Social Security: 24%
- Medicare, Medicaid, CHIP and Marketplace Subsidies: 24%
- Safety Net Programs: 11%
- Interest on Debt: 7%
- Benefits for Federal Retirees and Veterans: 8%
- Transportation Infrastructure: 3%
- Education: 2%
- Science and Medical Research: 2%
- Non-security International: 1%

The main issue is how to set income tax policy to be fair to the various income earning groups. What tax rate should be paid by the poor, working class, middle class, affluent, rich, and ultra-rich citizens? The poor generally pay no tax, and the working class pay a low tax rate. Today the highest marginal tax rate for the rich and ultra-rich is 39.4% (and a temporary 4% addition). Under President Eisenhower the highest tax rate was 90%, and under President Kennedy it went down to 70%. The question is whether the marginal tax rate for the rich and ultra-rich should be raised higher, say to 50 or 60%.

The Republicans always favor lowering the income tax rate and all taxes, not raising them. They think that the rich pay too high a marginal tax rate. Democrats, on the contrary, believe that taxes have to be raised higher on the rich and lower on the middle class and the working class. The Democrats also favor increasing the estate tax on the rich to reduce the growing wealth gap and the tendency toward plutocracy.

Here are the possible income tax policy alternatives:

- Leave the present tax system the way it is.
- Reduce taxes for everyone by introducing a flat tax at a low rate, such as 20%. This is highly favored by Republicans but it will necessitate cutting social programs.
- Increase the marginal tax rate for the very rich from 39.4% to somewhere between 50 and 60%. This is highly favored by Democrats.
- Reduce the middle class income tax rate and increase the rich income tax rate.
- Raise the estate tax rates more progressively after exempting the first $10 million for a married couple.

CONCLUSION

Many people around the world greatly admire the American model of democracy. The story of the American Revolution and the brilliant individuals who launched U.S. democracy—George Washington, Benjamin Franklin, Thomas Jefferson, John Adams, Alexander Hamilton, and many others—have inspired worldwide admiration and respect. People see in the history of American democracy a dynamism, a creativity, a respect for individual and human rights, a capacity to solve problems and invent new ones.

Yet there are forces and developments that are now testing the resilience of American democracy. America has produced great wealth but this wealth has not been shared by enough Americans. Citizens are questioning whether they are running the country or whether the '1%' are running the country. Our politicians need so much money to run their campaigns that they become beholden to the interests of wealthy corporations and individuals. The country's dynamism is becoming paralyzed by gridlock, gerrymandering, and excessive lobbying. Extreme elements have entered one or both political parties that have no interest in collaborating and compromising.

In this chapter I described a large number of major economic, political and social problems that remain unsolved and unresolved. The solutions are many and normal discourse between the adversaries would lead to their resolution. The solutions would benefit millions of citizens and keep democracy young and vital.

The solutions would not only benefit American citizens but provide an inspiration to other democracies around the world. Democracy contains self-corrective processes wherever its citizens are involved and their voices and rights are heard and respected. Democracy remains the only political system that promises to deliver in a pluralistic world a dynamic balance of liberty, egalitarianism, and compassion.

NOTE

1   https://en.wikipedia.org/wiki/Roe_v._Wade (accessed 03.03.16).

INDEX

Obamacare. *See* Affordable Care Act
 (ACA, 2010)
Occupy Wall Street movement, 7, 30–31
Of the Social Contract (Rousseau), 20–21
Ohio, 56
Oklahoma, 56, 117
Oregon, 119–120
originalism, 105, 109, 112
Ornstein, Norman, 127, 131

PACs and Super PACs (political action
 committees)
 control of, 53–55, 128, 186
 growth of, 132–133
 history of, 51–52
 role of, 24–25, 50, 52–53, 80–81, 185–186
 Sanders and, 5
 See also Citizens United v. FEC
Paine, Thomas, 21
Painter, Richard, 55
Pakistan, 143
Palestine, 144
Palin, Sarah, 91
Panama, 146
Paraguay, 146
parliamentary systems, 19, 25–26
Pelosi, Nancy, 132
Pendleton Act (1883), 50–51
Pericles, 38
Perot, H. Ross, 126
Pew Research Center, 30, 132
Philippines, 142
Plato, 19
plutocracy, 17
Pocan, Mark, 63
polarization, 127–133
political advertising, 133–134
political candidates, 44–48, 167–168. *See also*
 primaries
political institutions, 28–29
political parties
 candidates and, 44–46
 polarization and, 127–133
 political advertising and, 133–134
 role of, 125–127
 See also Democratic Party (U.S.); gridlock;
  Republican Party (U.S.)
poll taxes, 40

pollution, 186–187
popular vote, 55–56
pork barreling, 72–73, 82–83
Portugal, 144
post-democracy, 9
poverty, 3, 7, 168, 195–196
Powell, Colin, 146
President of the United States
 attitude toward, 89–90
 bureaucracy and, 98
 Congress and, 23, 29, 93, 94–97, 99,
  173–174
 foreign policy and, 146–147, 177
 impeachment of, 94
 legislative process and, 69, 94–95
 powers of, 90, 92–93
 qualifications of, 90–92
 responsibilities of, 90, 93–94
 salary of, 91
 See also specific presidents
Presidential Commission on Election
 Administration, 43
presidential systems, 23–25, 26
primaries
 Democratic Party and, 48
 polarization and, 172–173
 Republican Party and, 4–5, 39, 46–47, 48
 selection of candidates and, 46–48
 See also campaign finance; *specific candidates*
The Prince (Machiavelli), 19
prisons and incarceration, 31, 188, 192–193
pro-choice and pro-life groups, 108, 184–185
Prohibition, 177
Prohibition Party, 44
proportional representative (PR) system, 57
public sector
 citizen service in, 152–153
 citizens' view of, 29–31, 152
 good practices in, 155–161, *156*, 178–179
 improvement of operational performance
  in, 153–155
public transportation, 152. *See also* airports
Putin, Vladimir, 6, 144

Queensland, Australia, 157–158

race, 37
radio, 41, 133